ANIMALS AND THEIR HABITATS

Deserts and Scrublands

WORLD BOOK

A Scott Fetzer company
Chicago
www.worldbookonline.com

World Book, Inc.
233 N. Michigan Avenue
Chicago, IL 60601
U.S.A.

For information about other World Book publications, visit our website at http://www.worldbookonline.com or call 1-800-WORLDBK (967-5325).

For information about sales to schools and libraries, call 1-800-975-3250 (United States), or 1-800-837-5365 (Canada).

© 2012 World Book, Inc. All rights reserved. This volume may not be reproduced in whole or in part in any form without prior written permission from the publisher.

WORLD BOOK and the GLOBE DEVICE are registered trademarks or trademarks of World Book, Inc.

Staff

Executive Committee
President: Donald D. Keller
Vice President and Editor in Chief: Paul A. Kobasa
Vice President, Marketing/Digital Products: Sean Klunder
Vice President, International: Richard Flower
Controller: Yan Chen
Director, Human Resources: Bev Ecker

Editorial

Associate Director, Supplementary Publications:
  Scott Thomas
Managing Editor, Supplementary Publications:
  Barbara A. Mayes
Associate Manager, Supplementary Publications:
  Cassie Mayer
Editors: Brian Johnson and Kristina Vaicikonis
Researcher: Annie Brodsky
Editorial Assistant: Ethel Matthews
Manager, Contracts & Compliance
  (Rights & Permissions): Loranne K. Shields
Indexer: David Pofelski
Writer: David Alderton
Project Editor: Sarah Uttridge
Editorial Assistant: Kieron Connolly
Design: Andrew Easton

Graphics and Design

Senior Manager: Tom Evans
Senior Designer: Don Di Sante
Manager, Cartography: Wayne K. Pichler
Senior Cartographer: John Rejba

Pre-Press and Manufacturing

Director: Carma Fazio
Manufacturing Manager: Steven K. Hueppchen
Senior Production Manager: Janice Rossing
Production/Technology Manager: Anne Fritzinger
Proofreader: Emilie Schrage

Library of Congress Cataloging-in-Publication Data

Deserts and scrublands.
    p. cm. -- (Animals and their habitats)
  Includes index.
  Summary: "A highly illustrated introduction to many of the animals that live in the world's desert and scrubland regions. Detailed captions describe each animal, while inset maps show where the animals can be found around the world. Features include a glossary, maps, photographs, and an index" --Provided by publisher.
  ISBN 978-0-7166-0445-7
  1. Desert animals--Juvenile literature. 2. Desert ecology--Juvenile literature. I. World Book, Inc.
  QL116.D476 2012
  591.754--dc23
                2012005834

Animals and Their Habitats
Set ISBN: 978-0-7166-0441-9

Printed in China by Leo Paper Products, LTD.,
Heshan, Guangdong
1st printing July 2012

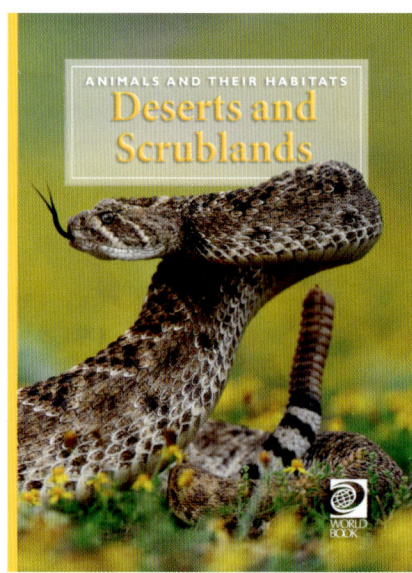

Cover image: The western diamond-back rattlesnake and other reptiles thrive in the hot, dry climate of the desert. Like many other desert creatures, the snake searches for food at night to escape the blistering rays of the sun.

© Rolf Nussbaumer, Nature Picture Library

Contents

Introduction 4

Habitat Map 5

Mammals (sheep, dingoes, and their relatives) 6

Birds (secretary-bird) 35

Arachnids (scorpions and spiders) 36

Insects (dung beetles) 41

Reptiles (lizards and rattlesnakes) 42

Glossary 46

Resources 47

Acknowledgments 47

Index 48

Introduction

A desert is one of the harshest environments on Earth. Little rain falls in deserts—generally an average of less than 10 inches (25 centimeters) a year. In some deserts, there may be no rain at all for several years. Deserts become scorching during the day as the temperature climbs. They grow cold at night as the temperature plummets. Only the hardiest animals and plants can live in a desert habitat. (A habitat is the kind of place in which an animal lives.)

The Sahara of North Africa is the world's largest desert. It extends over an area of about 3.5 million square miles (9 million square kilometers), stretching across a dozen different countries. There also are deserts in Australia, central Asia, South America, southern Africa, and southwestern North America. Desert areas in general occupy about one-fifth of the world's total land area.

Desert animals have *adaptations* (characteristics) that enable them to survive in harsh desert conditions. Because there is little rainfall, many desert animals get all the water they need from the food they eat. Some animals adapt to desert conditions in other ways. For example, the fennec fox has large ears that give off heat, helping the animal to cool its blood. The fox's paws are covered with fur, which provides protection from hot sand. Many desert animals are skilled diggers. Sheltering in *burrows* (underground shelters) enables these animals to escape the sun when it is at its hottest. Burrows also offer protection from *predators* (hunting animals). Most burrowing animals come out as the sun sets and the temperature cools. Harsh desert conditions have pushed some animals to extremes. The naked mole-rat lives entirely underground, in large *colonies* (groups) with up to 300 members. These colonies resemble ant colonies, with all the members under the rule of a large naked mole-rat queen.

NAKED MOLE-RAT

GILA MONSTER

INTRODUCTION 5

DESERTS AND SCRUBLANDS

SECRETARY-BIRD

Many kinds of animals live in deserts. Reptiles are common. Some of the world's most *venomous* (poisonous) snakes live in desert areas. The Gila monster, another desert reptile, is one of the world's only venomous lizards. Insects, scorpions, and spiders thrive in deserts. Many rodents and small mammals, such as rabbits and kangaroo rats, are desert animals. These animals provide food for such desert predators as birds of prey, jackals, and dingoes.

A scrubland is similar to a desert, but the conditions in this habitat are not as harsh. Rocky upland areas are common in scrublands. There, mountain sheep and similar animals dart from one rocky outcrop to another. Scrublands are also home to such larger mammals as the dromedary camel.

Gundi

SPECIES • *Ctenodactylus gundi*

VITAL STATISTICS	
WEIGHT	6–7 oz (170–190 g); females are slightly heavier
LENGTH	6–9 in (15–23 cm)
SEXUAL MATURITY	8–12 months
LENGTH OF PREGNANCY	25–30 days; births occur in the summer
NUMBER OF OFFSPRING	2; weaning by 4 weeks
DIET	Eats most of the plants in its native habitat
LIFESPAN	Up to 6 years; 10 in captivity

The kidneys of these rodents are so efficient at conserving water that they take in all the fluid they need from their food and do not have to drink regularly.

WHERE IN THE WORLD?

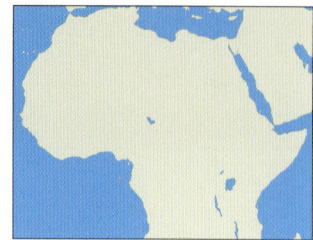

Gundis live in North Africa, from Algeria and Morocco southward to such countries as Niger, Chad, and Ethiopia.

ANIMAL FACTS
Gundis inhabit rocky areas of deserts. They live in *colonies* (groups) of as many as 100 individuals. Instead of building *burrows* (underground dens) or other shelters, gundis live in the crevices between rocks. The animals *forage* (search) for food beginning at daybreak. They pause around midday, then forage again in the late afternoon and evening. At night, they hide away in rocks. Individuals that feel threatened by *predators* (hunting animals) may play dead, as some predators refuse to eat dead animals. Mothers wean their young after only four weeks, probably because milk is difficult to produce in the dryness of the desert.

Bristles on the two inner toes of the hind feet are used like a brush for grooming.

EARS — These are flat and set low on the head. They do not move.

FUR — This is surprisingly dense and thick. The fur helps keep the animal warm at night, when the desert is cold.

PAWS — Bristles above their paws help the gundi when digging in sand.

TIGHT SQUEEZE — These rodents can flatten their bodies to fit into tight crevices in the rocks.

HOW BIG IS IT?

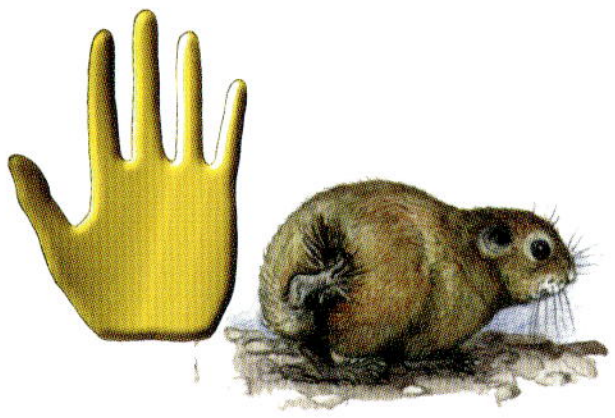

COAT CARE
Gundis have a distinctive grooming posture. They use a hind leg for this purpose while balancing on their other legs.

Lesser Egyptian Jerboa

SPECIES • *Jaculus jaculus*

VITAL STATISTICS	
WEIGHT	1.2–2.3 oz (33–65 g)
LENGTH	4–5 in (10–12 cm), not including the long tail
SEXUAL MATURITY	Females from 25 days, males from 45 days
LENGTH OF PREGNANCY	21 days; up to 17 litters a year recorded
NUMBER OF OFFSPRING	6–7, but can range from 2–9; weaning at 14 days
DIET	Eats grasses, herbs, seeds, fruit, and bark, as well as animal matter
LIFESPAN	1 year

Living in one of the harshest environments on the planet, lesser Egyptian jerboas are well equipped to survive in the searing heat of the desert.

WHERE IN THE WORLD?

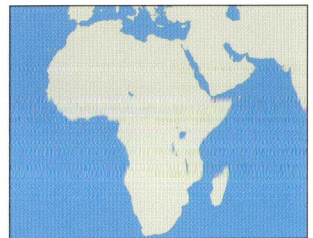

Lives in parts of North Africa, across the Arabian Peninsula and into Iran.

ANIMAL FACTS

These rodents are well suited to moving across the desert sand without becoming an easy target for *predators* (hunting animals). Jerboas usually walk on their long hind legs, which also help them to get a better view of their surroundings. When chased, jerboas can hop along quickly, covering distances of 10 feet (3 meters) in a single bound. They build a variety of *burrows* (underground shelters), including nesting sites. The entrances are hidden with sand. Most burrows include an emergency exit that is only lightly covered. This enables the jerboa to flee the burrow if a hungry snake enters.

TAIL
The long tail acts as a counterbalance when the jerboa jumps. It has a dark tip, often with a white patch.

EYES
The large eyes help them to quickly spot possible danger.

FRONT LEGS
These are short and are used only for holding food and grooming.

HIND FEET
Jerboas that are native to Africa have three toes on each foot. Asian *species* (kinds) have five toes on each foot.

HOW BIG IS IT?

BREEDING
Young jerboas are raised in underground nests by their mother. They are helpless at birth, with their eyes closed.

8 MAMMALS

Libyan Jird

SPECIES • *Meriones libycus*

VITAL STATISTICS	
WEIGHT	3.5 oz (100 g)
LENGTH	12 in (30 cm), including a tail as long as the body
SEXUAL MATURITY	About 3 months
LENGTH OF PREGNANCY	Around 26 days; 2 litters a year
NUMBER OF OFFSPRING	3–5; weaning occurs at 4 weeks
DIET	Eats bulbs, pods with seeds, and other plant matter; can cause crop damage
LIFESPAN	Up to 5 years

Closely related to gerbils, Libyan jirds communicate in a similar way—by drumming their hind legs on the ground as a warning of danger.

WHERE IN THE WORLD?

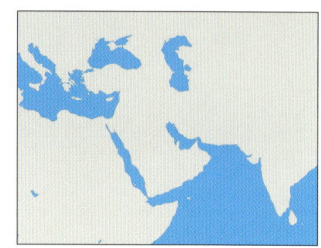

Ranges throughout Libya and Egypt's western desert, through the Middle East, via Israel, Jordan, Syria, and Saudi Arabia to Iran, Iraq, Afghanistan, Pakistan, and Azerbaijan.

ANIMAL FACTS

The behavior of these rodents varies across their range. In some places, they are active aboveground during the day. Elsewhere, they are strictly *nocturnal* (active at night). This behavior may be influenced by *predators* (hunting animals) in the area. For example, in areas with hawks—which hunt during the day—jirds are likely to be more active after dark. Libyan jirds usually live in *colonies* (groups). In winter, jirds in some areas may sleep in their *burrows* (underground shelters) for certain periods to avoid harsh weather.

EARS
Sharp hearing is vital for the survival of these rodents, which live in open countryside.

EYES
The eyes are large, helping the jird to see in poor conditions.

WHISKERS
These help them sense their surroundings while tunneling or hiding under rocks.

TAIL
This acts as a counterbalance when the jird is sitting on its hindquarters and when it jumps.

VISITORS NOT WELCOME
Jirds often construct their burrows under piles of vegetation, hiding the entrance from predators.

SURVIVAL IN THE DESERT
The jird's kidneys produce a concentrated urine, helping the animal to survive in areas where water can be scarce.

Jirds eat using their paws to hold food.

HOW BIG IS IT?

MAMMALS 9

Naked Mole-Rat

SPECIES • *Heterocephalus glaber*

These bizarre rodents are well suited to life underground. They have narrow bodies and short legs. Their social structure is similar to that of such insects as ants and bees.

VITAL STATISTICS	
WEIGHT	1–2.8 oz (30–80 g); queens are significantly larger than workers
LENGTH	3.1–3.9 in (8–10 cm)
SEXUAL MATURITY	6–12 months
LENGTH OF PREGNANCY	66–74 days
NUMBER OF OFFSPRING	3–12, but can be up to 27 pups per litter, with queens having up to 4 litters a year
DIET	Feeds on roots and vegetation
LIFESPAN	Up to 25 years in captivity

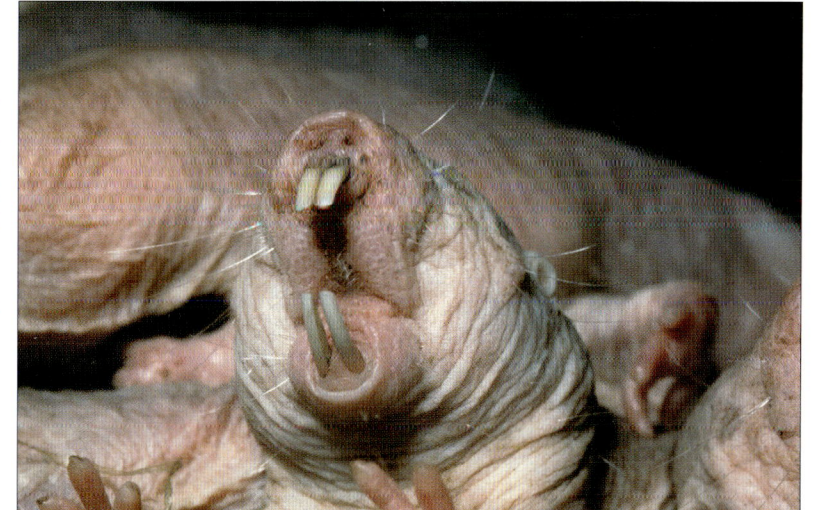

WHERE IN THE WORLD?

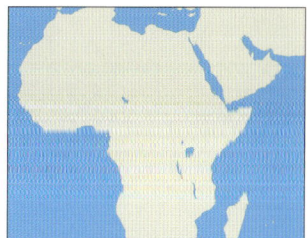

Lives in East Africa, mainly in southern Ethiopia, Somalia, and Kenya.

ANIMAL FACTS

There can be up to 300 mole-rats in a *colony* (group). The colony is organized around a ruling female, much like the queen in an ant colony. She is the only female who breeds. She bullies other females to prevent their development. If the queen dies, another female soon takes her place. All the other mole-rats work for the colony. Some grow larger and defend the colony from snakes and other *predators* (hunting animals). These animals may sacrifice themselves for the sake of the colony.

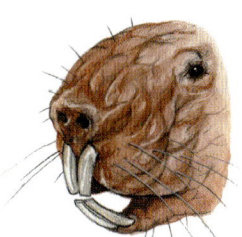

The lips of the naked mole-rat close behind their *incisors* (cutting teeth). This helps the animal to dig without getting dirt in its mouth.

BODY
The skin is largely hairless, apart from some longer whisker-like hairs around the mouth and body.

EYES
These are tiny and almost nonfunctional, though they can detect light.

EARS
The earflaps are very small.

TEETH
The large, protruding incisors in the upper and lower jaws extend over the lips.

Tuber

UNDERGROUND LIVING
Mole-rats live in a series of interconnecting tunnels, seeking out *tubers* (underground stems) in the sandy soil. The tubers may sometimes be stored in a burrow.

HOW BIG IS IT?

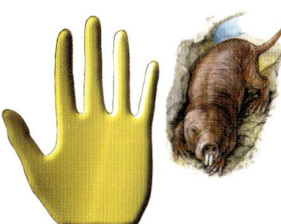

TUNNELING
Mole-rats bite into the hard soil and then scoop it out of the burrow with their legs.

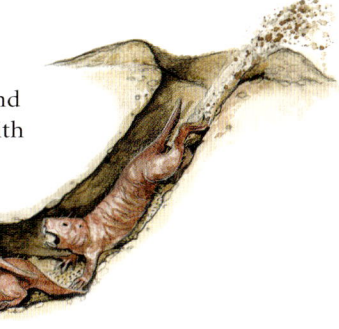

Dorcas Gazelle

SPECIES • *Gazella dorcas*

VITAL STATISTICS	
Weight	33–44 lb (15–20 kg)
Length	36–48 in (55–65 cm), including tail
Sexual Maturity	Females 9 months; males 1.5 years
Length of Pregnancy	About 186 days; young then conceal themselves for up to 6 weeks
Number of Offspring	A single youngster, occasionally 2; weaned by 3 months
Diet	Eats grasses, leaves, and desert plants
Lifespan	12 years maximum

Graceful and fast, these gazelles are well suited to life in the desert. They can go for years without drinking water, obtaining water from dew and the food they eat.

WHERE IN THE WORLD?

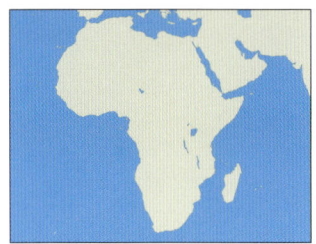

Present throughout northern parts of Africa, down through the Horn of Africa and east across the Arabian Peninsula.

ANIMAL FACTS

To find food, these gazelles often travel long distances to areas where rain has fallen recently. The sexes frequently form separate herds. Males are territorial, especially during the mating season. They use dung and urine to mark their *territories* (personal areas). When the gazelles sense danger, they make a duck-like quack through the nose. The nose inflates temporarily while producing the sound. Numbers of these gazelles are falling, mainly because of overhunting for their meat and horns.

The tail is used for signaling.

Nature
Gazelles are gentle animals. The name *gazelle* comes from an Arabic word that means *to be affectionate*.

Coat
Their pale color blends in with their sandy environment, providing camouflage. Their white underparts may reflect heat.

Male horns
Horns of the male are more curved and larger than those of the female, growing up to 15 inches (38 centimeters) in length.

Ears
Large ears help detect sound in the still desert environment.

Female horns
Females have narrower, straighter horns, which measure 10 inches (25 centimeters) in length.

HOW BIG IS IT?

STAYING ALIVE

Living where there is no cover, dorcas gazelles must rely on their grace and speed to escape *predators* (hunting animals).

Barbary Sheep

SPECIES • *Ammotragus lervia*

These sheep are named after their native area, which was once known as the Barbary States for the people who live there. Barbary sheep are the only sheep native to Africa.

VITAL STATISTICS

WEIGHT	Females average 88–110 lb (40–55 kg); males average 220–320 lb (100–145 kg)
LENGTH	4.5–5.5 ft (1.3–1.6 m); females are smaller
SEXUAL MATURITY	2 years
LENGTH OF PREGNANCY	About 5 ½ months
NUMBER OF OFFSPRING	1–2 lambs, occasionally 3; ewes may produce two litters annually
DIET	Eats scrubby desert vegetation, including acacia shrubs and lichens
LIFESPAN	About 10 years in the wild; 20 years in captivity

WHERE IN THE WORLD?

Lives in the mountainous area of the western Sahara, extending to Egypt and Sudan. Has also been introduced to Spain and parts of the United States, including Texas.

ANIMAL FACTS

Because they live in areas with little natural cover, Barbary sheep rely on the color of their coats to avoid detection. If necessary, these sheep can jump up to 6 feet (1.8 meters) to escape danger. Males battle each other ferociously at the start of the breeding season, though these fights are largely trials of strength.

Climbing a cliff face

COLORATION
Mainly sandy brown, darkening with age.

HORNS
These grow away from the head and then curve inward, reaching up to 20 inches (50 centimeters) in length.

BEARD
Only the male has this trailing shaggy area of hair extending down from the lower jaw onto the chest.

HOOFS
The *cloven* (split) hoofs provide support when the sheep is climbing on rocky surfaces.

HOW BIG IS IT?

HEAD FOR HEIGHTS
Barbary sheep often shelter on the rocky ledges of difficult-to-reach cliffs to avoid the heat of the desert sun at midday.

Arabian Oryx

SPECIES • *Oryx leucoryx*

VITAL STATISTICS

Weight	143–154 lb (65–70 kg)
Length	4–5 ft (1.2–1.5 m), including tail
Sexual Maturity	1.5–2 years
Length of Pregnancy	255–270 days
Number of Offspring	1; weaning occurs after 3 ½ months
Diet	Grazes on grass and browses on leaves and shoots
Lifespan	Up to 20 years in captivity; shorter in the wild

ANIMAL FACTS

The case of the Arabian oryx is a conservation success story. The species was hunted to extinction in the wild after World War II (1939-1945), finally disappearing in 1972. Luckily, there were some 500 of the animals in zoos. Thanks to captive breeding programs, the animal has been reintroduced to parts of its former range, starting in 1982. Arabian oryxes continue to be released in the United Arab Emirates as part of a plan to return 500 of the animals to the wild by 2012.

The Arabian oryx *(AWR ihks)* is known for its ability to detect rainfall from great distances. The herd will travel toward the rainfall in search of new plant growth.

WHERE IN THE WORLD?

Range once extended through Syria, Iraq, Jordan, Israel, and the Arabian Peninsula. Reintroduced to the wild in several countries, including Jordan, Oman, and the United Arab Emirates.

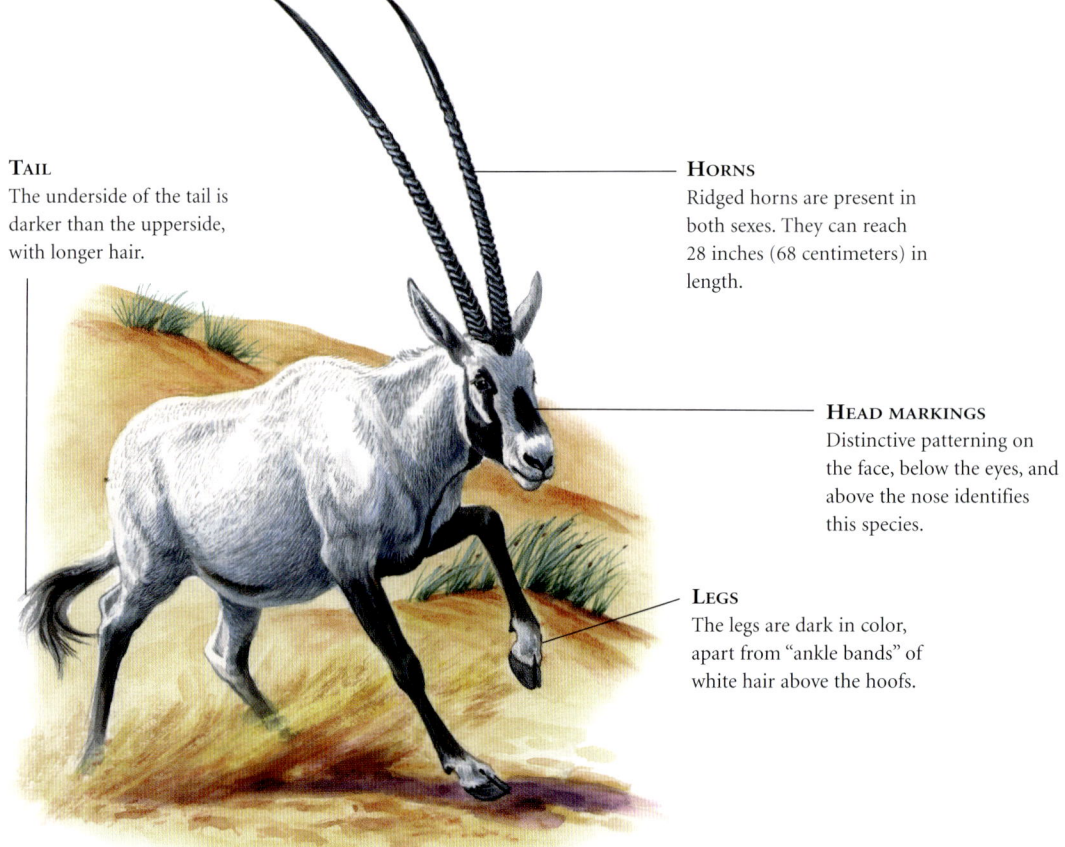

Tail
The underside of the tail is darker than the upperside, with longer hair.

Horns
Ridged horns are present in both sexes. They can reach 28 inches (68 centimeters) in length.

Head markings
Distinctive patterning on the face, below the eyes, and above the nose identifies this species.

Legs
The legs are dark in color, apart from "ankle bands" of white hair above the hoofs.

Drinking at a water hole

HOW BIG IS IT?

POSTURING

In spite of their fierce appearance, Arabian oryx are not aggressive. They communicate mainly through the position of their horns.

MAMMALS 13

Argali (Mountain Sheep)

SPECIES • *Ovis ammon*

The argali is the largest species of wild sheep in the world, standing 47 inches (120 centimeters) tall at the shoulder. Unfortunately, it is endangered.

VITAL STATISTICS	
WEIGHT	143–396 lb (65–180 kg)
LENGTH	53–84 in (134–214 cm), including tail
SEXUAL MATURITY	Females about 2 years; males 5 years
LENGTH OF PREGNANCY	150–160 days; weaning occurs at about 4 months
NUMBER OF OFFSPRING	Typically 1, although occasionally twins are born
DIET	Grazes on grass, sedges, and other vegetation
LIFESPAN	10–13 years

WHERE IN THE WORLD?

Lives throughout upland areas of central Asia and northern India, at altitudes of 4,200–19,500 feet (1,300–6,100 meters). Present in the Himalaya region, extending east to Mongolia.

ANIMAL FACTS

The name *argali* is the native Mongolian word for these sheep. Like all sheep, argalis are highly social animals and form single-sex herds of up to 100 individuals. In some areas, male argalis are hunted for sport. But the major threat to the survival of these sheep is loss of *habitat* (an area where an animal lives) to sheep raised by people. Argali herds also are targeted by wolves and snow leopards. Eagles and other birds of prey often carry off lambs. Mating occurs in the early winter. Females give birth the following spring.

HORNS
Males have huge corkscrew horns that can reach 75 inches (190 centimeters) in length overall. The horns of females are much smaller.

FACE
The face is completely white; small ears are located beneath the horns.

COLORATION
Color is variable, ranging from buff to grayish-brown on the upperparts and white on the underparts.

HOOFS
The hoofs ensure these sheep do not slip when climbing in their rocky habitat.

Argali live in single-sex groups when not breeding.

HOW BIG IS IT?

MATERNAL BEHAVIOR
An ewe separates from the herd to give birth. She and her offspring return after several days. A mother nurses her young for about four months.

14 MAMMALS

Bighorn Sheep

SPECIES • *Ovis canadensis*

VITAL STATISTICS	
Weight	117–279 lb (53–127 kg)
Length	5–6 ft (1.5–1.8 m), including tail
Sexual Maturity	Females about 2.5 years; males about 3 years, but often do not breed until they are older
Length of Pregnancy	About 175 days; weaning occurs at 4–6 months
Number of Offspring	1
Diet	Grazes mainly on grass but also on herbs and other small plants
Lifespan	Up to 14 years

Bighorn sheep live in mountainous areas throughout their large range. Individual bighorn sheep populations tend to remain in a certain area rather than mixing together.

WHERE IN THE WORLD?

Lives in North America, mainly in the Rocky Mountains, extending from British Columbia and Alberta in western Canada to eastern parts of Baja California.

ANIMAL FACTS

Bighorn sheep are extremely sure-footed and can climb and jump with grace. These abilities are vital for an animal that lives in mountain regions. A surprising characteristic of these sheep is that they are strong swimmers. Horn size plays a key role in the social structure of bighorn sheep. Males with the largest horns are unchallenged. When two males are well matched in horn size, they must battle for their place in the social ranking of the herd.

FEMALE HORNS Female horns are slimmer and far less developed than those of the male.

MALE HORNS The horns of the male are massive, growing backward and then curling forward toward the face.

COAT The brownish coloration of the body varies between different populations.

Young bighorn sheep lie down to avoid eagles and other *predators* (hunting animals).

HOW BIG IS IT?

HORN GROWTH The horns grow gradually in the male. A second curl may start to develop when the animal is about 8 years old.

Mouflon

SPECIES • *Ovis aries*

This vulnerable *species* (kind) of wild sheep is one of the original ancestors of today's *domesticated* (tamed) sheep. People began breeding sheep from 7,000 to 11,000 years ago in southwestern Asia.

VITAL STATISTICS

WEIGHT	89–110 lb (35–50 kg); males are heavier
LENGTH	50–77 in (127–195 cm), including tail; up to 35 in (90 cm) tall
SEXUAL MATURITY	1 year, but may not breed for another 2 years
LENGTH OF PREGNANCY	148–155 days
NUMBER OF OFFSPRING	1–2; weaning at around 120–150 days
DIET	Grazes on vegetation including grass and small plants in pasture
LIFESPAN	Up to 20 years

WHERE IN THE WORLD?

Lives in Europe, including Cyprus and Sardinia, and southwest Asia, extending through parts of Iran and the Caucasus region.

ANIMAL FACTS

These wild sheep inhabit dry, mountainous areas. *Rams* (males) live on their own, but *ewes* (females) mingle in flocks with their young. It takes up to nine years for the horns of rams to reach their maximum size. By then, they can weigh up to 11 pounds (5 kilograms). The skull beneath is reinforced with extra bone, giving greater protection for the mating season, when fighting is likely to break out between males. Mouflon can breed with domestic sheep.

Mouflon rams in combat

SIZE This is one of the smaller kinds of wild sheep.

COLORATION The ewe is more evenly colored than the ram.

EYES The irises are yellow. These sheep are known for their good vision.

HORNS The horns curl backward then forward and are present only in males.

APPEARANCE Rams are a rich, dark reddish-brown color with a short, glossy coat that thickens in the winter.

A FIRST CLONING SUCCESS

The number of mouflon has fallen because of overhunting, breeding with domestic sheep, and loss of *habitat* (area where an animal lives). In 2001, scientists successfully cloned a mouflon, which may help preserve the species.

HOW BIG IS IT?

Bactrian Camel

SPECIES • *Camelus bactrianus*

VITAL STATISTICS	
WEIGHT	1,320–2,200 lb (600–1,000 kg)
LENGTH	10 ft (3 m), including tail; stands up to 7 ft (2 m) tall
SEXUAL MATURITY	Females 3–4 years; males 5–6 years
LENGTH OF PREGNANCY	About 365–430 days; weaning occurs at 1–2 years
NUMBER OF OFFSPRING	1, occasionally 2
DIET	Grazes on grass and browses on taller plants
LIFESPAN	Up to 40 years

The *domestication* (taming) of these camels began more than 4,500 years ago. Today, there are more than 2 million domestic Bactrian camels, but the wild population is highly endangered.

WHERE IN THE WORLD?

Once found across much of Asia, they now remain only in western China and Mongolia.

ANIMAL FACTS

Camels live in harsh environments and are exposed to extremes of temperature throughout the year. So it is not surprising that the Bactrian camel's dense winter coat may fall off in huge chunks as the weather changes. Camels are often described as "ships of the desert," partly because of their rolling gait. This results from their unusual way of walking, with both legs on one side of the body moving forward together, followed by the legs on the other side.

BEARD
A long beard runs down the underside of the throat, with hairs up to 10 inches (25 centimeters) long.

HUMPS
The humps store fat. Their shape indicates the camel's condition. A well-fed camel has upright humps that do not slope to the side.

GETTING UP
To rise from the ground, camels raise their hindquarters and then push themselves up with their forelegs.

FEET
Both toes on each foot spread out as the camel walks, preventing it from sinking into sand.

Long eyelashes keep sand out of the camel's eyes.

HOW BIG IS IT?

VERSATILE COMPANIONS

Camels are valued not only for carrying goods in packs slung over their bodies but also providing milk.

Dromedary Camel

SPECIES • *Camelus dromedarius*

VITAL STATISTICS	
WEIGHT	550–1,600 lb (250–725 kg)
LENGTH	138 in (350 cm), including tail; up to 7 ft (2 m) tall
SEXUAL MATURITY	Females 3–4 years; males 5–6 years
LENGTH OF PREGNANCY	About 365–400 days; weaning occurs at 1–2 years
NUMBER OF OFFSPRING	1, occasionally 2
DIET	Grazes on grass and browses on taller plants
LIFESPAN	Up to 40 years

This species mostly died out in the wild about 2,000 years ago. All dromedaries today are the descendants of *domesticated* (tamed) stock. Their population is estimated at about 15 million.

WHERE IN THE WORLD?

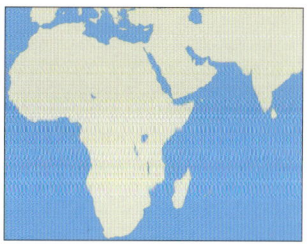

Found throughout northern Africa to the Horn of Africa and through Arabia and the Middle East to northwestern India. Has been introduced to parts of central Australia.

ANIMAL FACTS

Dromedaries, also known as Arabian camels, are amazingly well *adapted* (suited) to desert life. They can survive for long periods without drinking. They convert the fat in their humps to water and energy when water is scarce. They can also get fluid from plants. When they drink, dromedaries can consume up to 30 gallons (135 liters) of water at one time.

Dromedary, or Arabian, camel

Bactrian camel

HUMPS
Dromedaries have a large hump in the middle of their back. They have a second hidden hump that sits over the shoulders.

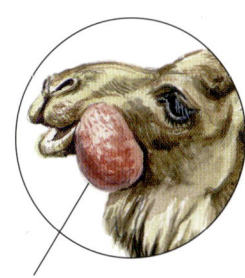

BALLOONING TISSUE
Male dromedaries inflate their soft *palate* (roof of the mouth) and hang it out of their mouth to attract females during the mating season.

KNEES
Callouses of hard skin form on the camel's knees where it lies down.

SAND PROTECTION
Dromedaries have two rows of long eyelashes to shield their eyes from sand. They can also close their nostrils.

LEGENDARY TRAVELER
Long valued as pack animals, dromedaries can travel at a rate of about 10 miles (16 kilometers) an hour and cover 100 miles (160 kilometers) in a day.

HOW BIG IS IT?

UNDERSIDE OF THE FOOT
The two well-padded toes forming the foot absorb the camel's weight as it moves. There is a claw on each toe.

18 MAMMALS

African Wild Ass

SPECIES • *Equus africanus*

This wild *species* (kind) is the ancestor of the *domesticated* (tamed) donkey. They were domesticated more than 6,000 years ago. Unfortunately, wild asses have become endangered in recent years.

VITAL STATISTICS	
Weight	500–600 lb (230–275 kg)
Length	6.6 ft (2 m); tail up to 20 in (50 cm); up to 4.75 ft (1.45 m) tall
Sexual Maturity	2 years
Length of Pregnancy	11–12 months
Number of Offspring	1; weaning occurs at 6–8 months
Diet	Grazes on grasses and other plants; also eats bark and leaves
Lifespan	Up to 40 years

WHERE IN THE WORLD?

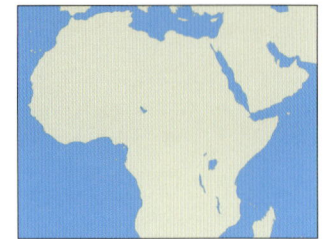

Northeastern Africa, now restricted to Eritrea, Ethiopia, and Somalia. Formerly ranged more widely to the west and north, reaching Libya, Sudan, and Egypt.

ANIMAL FACTS

Wild asses rest during the heat of the day and emerge in the late afternoon to feed and drink. Herds also move in the early morning. Males use their *dung* (solid waste) as territorial markers, but they tolerate the presence of younger stallions in their *territory* (personal areas). Only a few hundred of these animals remain in the wild. Hunting by people and interbreeding with domesticated donkeys have helped to push the African wild ass to the edge of *extinction* (disappearing totally).

Coloration
The animals are mostly gray with brown on the upperparts and white underparts. They have a black, upright mane running down the back of their head.

Ears
These are tall, helping the ass to detect sounds over long distances. They are edged with black hair.

Striping
The variable striped patterning on the neck is also apparent on the legs. The patterns differ from animal to animal.

Hoofs
The black hoofs are tough but slender and are about as wide as the leg.

Modern donkeys, such as this Poitou donkey, have been bred from African wild asses.

HOW BIG IS IT?

MALE COMBAT
Males fight each other by rearing up on their hind legs and lashing out with their front feet.

Coyote

SPECIES • *Canis latrans*

VITAL STATISTICS	
Weight	15–45 lb (7–21 kg); males are heavier, as are those of northern races
Length	3–4.5 ft (1–1.4 m); up to 1.5–2 ft (0.5–0.6 m) tall
Sexual Maturity	12 months
Length of Pregnancy	60–63 days
Number of Offspring	1–19, average 6; weaned by 35 days
Diet	Feeds mainly on small mammals, larger insects, and birds; also eats plant matter and animal remains
Lifespan	11–12 years

ANIMAL FACTS

Despite being widely hunted, coyotes have become numerous throughout North America. These relatively small and agile members of the dog family are unpopular with ranchers because they sometimes attack sheep, cattle, and other livestock. However, coyotes usually feed on such rodents as gophers and mice. They also eat jack rabbits, which can harm grazing pastures.

Increasingly, coyotes and human beings are sharing urban spaces. Coyotes are shy, so people rarely see them. But thousands of coyotes have moved into cities and suburbs.

WHERE IN THE WORLD?

Lives throughout North America, from Alaska south to Mexico. Absent only from north-central and western Canada.

EARS
The ears are broad. When held erect, they help pinpoint sounds, allowing the animal to hunt in the dark.

SNOUT
The snout is narrow, with black nostrils.

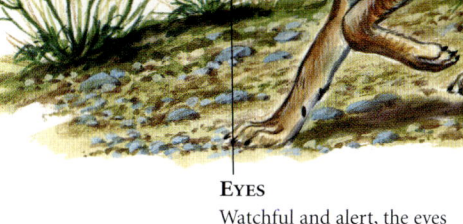

EYES
Watchful and alert, the eyes are green. Coyotes have excellent night vision.

COLORATION
Coyotes from desert areas have reddish coats, while those that live in woodland areas are more gray.

Coyotes feed on any animal they can take down, though porcupines are a challenge.

HOW BIG IS IT?

HOWLING AT THE MOON
Coyotes are known for their eerie howl, usually heard during the evening, night, or early morning.

Dingo

SPECIES • *Canis lupus dingo*

VITAL STATISTICS	
Weight	20–45 lb (9–20 kg); males are heavier
Length	3.5–4 ft (1.1–1.2 m); up to 23 in (58 cm) tall
Sexual Maturity	Females 2 years; males 1–3 years
Length of Pregnancy	61–69 days; weaned at 3–6 months
Number of Offspring	5–6
Diet	Feeds on rabbits, rats, possums, wallabies, kangaroos, sheep, calves, birds, reptiles, and animal remains
Lifespan	Up to 14 years

The ancestors of the dingo were brought to Australia many thousands of years ago by Aboriginal peoples. Now, these dogs live on the continent as wild animals.

WHERE IN THE WORLD?

The dingo lives only on the mainland of Australia.

ANIMAL FACTS

Dingoes are feral dogs, meaning they have changed from being *domesticated* (tamed) to being free-roaming. This has brought them into conflict with farmers because dingoes prey on sheep. But the dogs also benefit farmers by killing such pests as rabbits and wild pigs. Dingoes are mainly *nocturnal* (active at night). They live on their own or in small packs. Females have just one litter each year. They can also crossbreed successfully with domestic dogs.

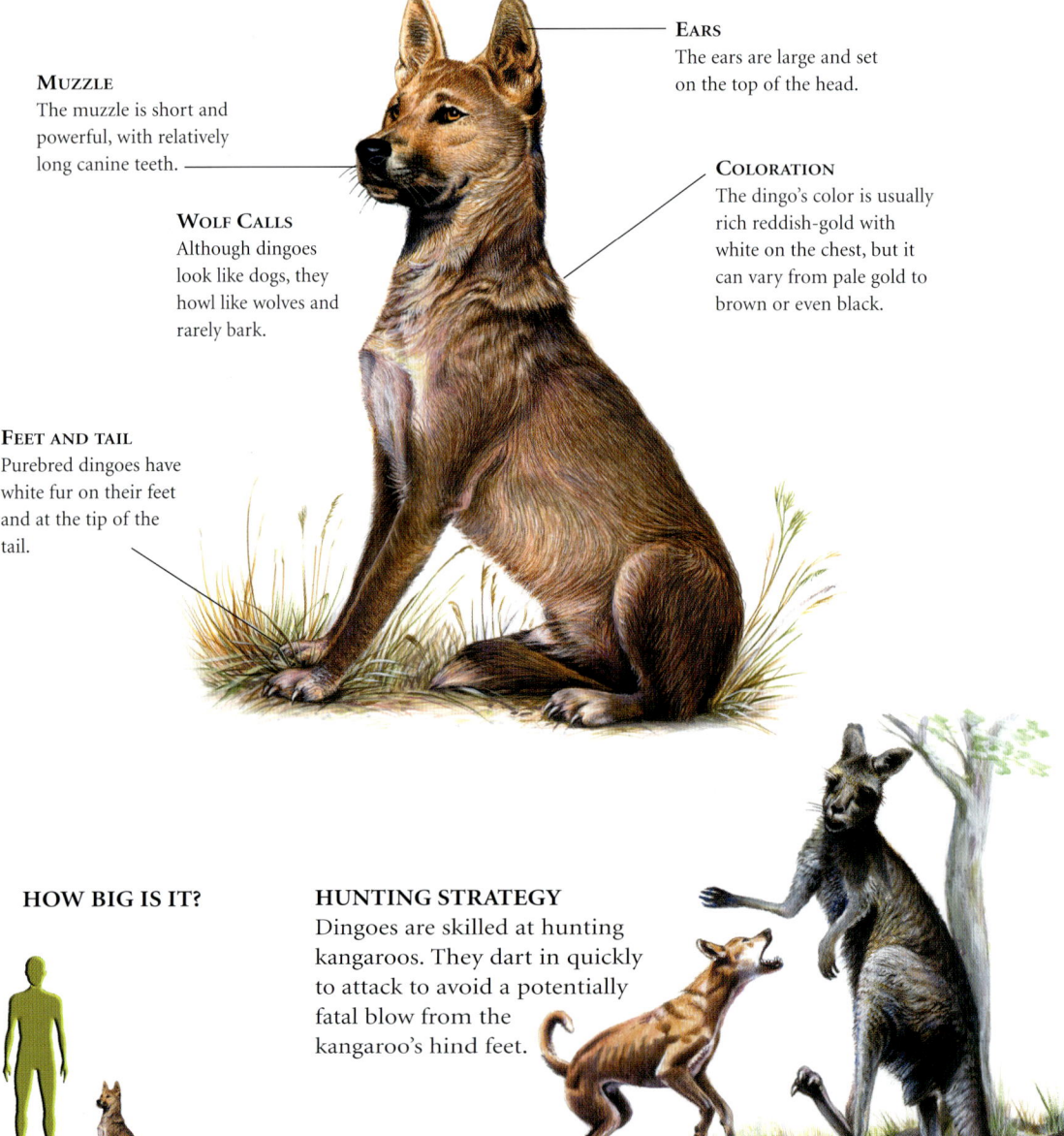

Muzzle The muzzle is short and powerful, with relatively long canine teeth.

Wolf Calls Although dingoes look like dogs, they howl like wolves and rarely bark.

Feet and tail Purebred dingoes have white fur on their feet and at the tip of the tail.

Ears The ears are large and set on the top of the head.

Coloration The dingo's color is usually rich reddish-gold with white on the chest, but it can vary from pale gold to brown or even black.

The dingo (left) was used to breed the Australian cattle dog (right).

HOW BIG IS IT?

HUNTING STRATEGY

Dingoes are skilled at hunting kangaroos. They dart in quickly to attack to avoid a potentially fatal blow from the kangaroo's hind feet.

Black-Backed Jackal

SPECIES • *Canis mesomelas*

Fossil evidence suggests that this species may be the oldest surviving member of the dog family, appearing before the gray wolf and long before the *domesticated* (tamed) dog.

VITAL STATISTICS

WEIGHT	15–30 lb (7–13.5 kg); males and southern races are heavier
LENGTH	37–54 in (95–136 cm); up to 19 in (42 cm) tall
SEXUAL MATURITY	About 11 months
LENGTH OF PREGNANCY	60–65 days
NUMBER OF OFFSPRING	3–6
DIET	Hunts mainly hares and rodents; also scavenges and eats fruit and berries
LIFESPAN	Up to 8 years in the wild; can be 12–14 years in captivity

WHERE IN THE WORLD?

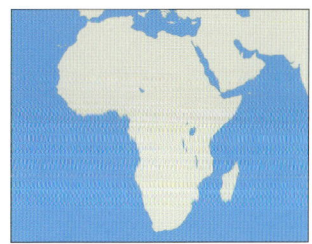

Two separate populations, one in eastern Africa, including Ethiopia, Kenya, and Somalia, and another across southern Africa, in Botswana, Namibia, South Africa, and Zimbabwe.

ANIMAL FACTS

Female black-backed jackals tend to be paler in color than males. Pairs form a lifelong bond. They sometimes join up with other black-backed jackals to hunt larger prey. Some of the young from the previous year may also stay with their parents, helping them to hunt and increasing the survival chances of the next set of offspring. Jackals are opportunistic—that is, they eat whatever food they can find.

Jackals will dig *burrows* (underground shelters) or use holes dug by other animals.

COLORATION
Silver-black fur runs the entire length of the back and tail, contrasting with the gingery flanks.

EARS
The animal's keen sense of hearing helps it to locate prey hidden by vegetation.

PROFILE
These jackals are slimmer than related species, as emphasized by their long muzzle.

WHISKERS
Whiskers help jackals learn about their environment, such as confirming the direction of the wind so their prey does not catch their scent while hunting.

HUNTING TOGETHER
Hunting partnerships can be very successful. Here, one jackal distracts the female gazelle, allowing the other jackal to seize her young.

HOW BIG IS IT?

Golden Jackal

SPECIES • *Canis aureus*

Jackals are wild dogs that live in Asia, Africa, and southeastern Europe. The golden jackal is the largest *species* (kind) of jackal, but it varies in size and color across its wide range.

VITAL STATISTICS	
Weight	15–33 lb (7–15 kg); males are heavier
Length	38–52 in (95–130 cm), including tail; up to 20 in (up to 50 cm) tall
Sexual Maturity	About 11 months
Length of Pregnancy	About 63 days; weaning occurs up to 3 months later
Number of Offspring	2–4
Diet	Hunts birds and mammals, scavenges, and eats plant matter
Lifespan	12–14 years

WHERE IN THE WORLD?

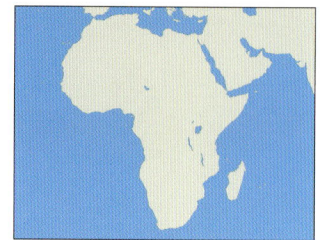

Found in northern and eastern parts of Africa, through Arabia and southern parts of Asia, east to Southeast Asia. Also lives in parts of southeastern Europe.

ANIMAL FACTS

Golden jackals are quite common throughout their range and are highly *adaptable* (flexible). In some regions, groups of up to five individuals may hunt together, which helps them to overpower larger and potentially faster prey. Their acute hearing also enables them to locate small animals hiding in vegetation. They can become skilled at catching fish. When prey are hard to find, they will eat insects and fruit.

COLORATION
The fur is usually yellowish with darker tipping, but this can vary both by season and region.

DEVELOPMENT OF PUPS
Pups weigh about 7 ounces (200 grams) at birth. Their eyes open when they are about 10 days old.

TAIL
The bushy tail is usually held down at rest.

Golden jackals playing

HOW BIG IS IT?

HELPERS
Young from a previous litter may stay with the adult pair, helping to protect new pups from intruders.

Fennec Fox

SPECIES • *Vulpes zerda*

VITAL STATISTICS	
Weight	2–3 lb (1–1.5 kg; males slightly larger
Length	17–28 in (43–71 cm); may stand 8 in (20 cm) tall
Sexual Maturity	6–11 months
Length of Pregnancy	50–52 days; weaning occurs at 8 weeks
Number of Offspring	2–5
Diet	Hunts rodents, rabbits, small birds, and lizards; also eats insects and fruit
Lifespan	Typically 9–11 years, but up to 16 years in captivity

These desert-dwelling foxes are superbly *adapted* (suited) to living in a harsh environment. They are the smallest kind of fox and the smallest member of the dog family, with unusually large ears for their size.

WHERE IN THE WORLD?

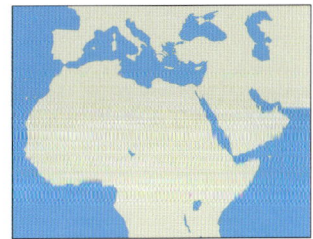

Restricted largely to the Sahara region of North Africa, living in Algeria, Egypt, Libya, Morocco, Sudan, and Tunisia. Also ranges northeast of the Red Sea.

ANIMAL FACTS

Fennecs communicate using a variety of calls, including growls and barks. They also have a distinctive purr, like a cat. Because their bodies lose water slowly, fennecs can go for days without drinking. They normally live in family groups of up to 10 individuals. They are highly territorial, marking their area with urine. They live in *burrows* (underground shelters), where the young are born in spring. The cubs start to venture above ground when at about a month old.

EARS
The ears are much larger than the head, measuring up to 6 inches (15 centimeters) in length.

COLORATION
The fennec's sandy color helps it stay cool in the daytime heat and to blend into the sand to avoid *predators* (hunting animals).

MUZZLE
The muzzle is short and narrow.

FEET
The paws are covered with fur, helping these foxes to walk on sand without burning the skin.

Female fennecs give birth to two to five young each spring.

HOW BIG IS IT?

HEAT LOSS
Fennec foxes stay cool by giving off heat through their large ears. Dogs give off heat by panting.

African Hunting Dog

SPECIES • *Lycaon pictus*

The scientific name of this animal translates as *painted wolf*. It refers to their highly individual patterning, which allows individuals to be identified from some distance away.

VITAL STATISTICS	
Weight	37–79 lb (17–36 kg); males slightly larger
Length	21–23 in (52–58 cm); up to 30 in (75 cm) tall
Sexual Maturity	12–18 months
Length of Pregnancy	65–70 days; weaning occurs at 10 weeks
Number of Offspring	2–19, but an average of 10
Diet	Hunts both medium-sized animals, such as impalas, and bigger animals, such as zebras and ostriches
Lifespan	Up to 11 years in the wild

WHERE IN THE WORLD?

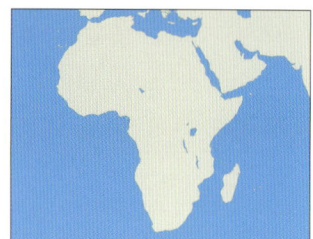

Confined to Africa, ranging across central and eastern parts of the continent, down to northern South Africa and northern Namibia.

Ears — Large and rounded at the tips, the ears are sensitive to a wide variety of sounds.

Toes — Unlike other *canids* (members of the dog family), African hunting dogs have only four toes on each front foot.

Coloration — Coats have black, red, yellow, brown, and white areas. No two individuals have the same markings.

Camouflage — The mottled coloring of these wild dogs helps them to blend in well in grassland areas.

ANIMAL FACTS

African hunting dogs live in *packs* (groups). The pack works together to hunt. They typically chase prey until it is too tired to continue running. Then they drag it down and feed. The pack also works together to raise young and provide food to sick dogs. Packs have grown smaller as African wild dogs have become less common. Smaller packs are less able to tackle such large prey as gazelles and wildebeests. African hunting dogs are now endangered, mainly because of hunting and disease.

HOLDING ON

When attacking prey, one member of the pack always holds on to the animal's tail, slowing down the animal and holding it in place so other members of the pack can strike.

A female feeds her litter by vomiting up partly digested food.

HOW BIG IS IT?

Sand Cat

SPECIES • *Felis margarita*

These small cats are hard to see because they stay in their *burrows* (underground shelters) during the day, coming out at night to hunt, and because their sandy brown coat blends well with their surroundings.

VITAL STATISTICS

WEIGHT	4.5–6.5 lb (2–3 kg)
LENGTH	17–22 in (45–57 cm); about 10 in (25 cm) tall
SEXUAL MATURITY	Around 14 months
LENGTH OF PREGNANCY	59–66 days
NUMBER OF OFFSPRING	Average 4–5, but can be up to 8; weaning at around 90 days
DIET	Feeds mainly on such desert rodents as jerboas; also birds, lizards, insects, and spiders
LIFESPAN	6–7 years in the wild; up to 13 in captivity

WHERE IN THE WORLD?

Lives in the Sahara region of North Africa, through the Middle East and Arabian Peninsula to Turkmenistan, Kazakhstan, and Pakistan.

ANIMAL FACTS

These small cats rely partly on their small size and coloration to hide themselves in a landscape where there is little natural cover. They also dig shallow *burrows* (underground shelters) in the sand, where they hide during the hottest part of the day. The long fur covering their pads helps protect their feet against the hot sand. Sand cats are solitary, and females give birth alone.

COLORATION
The coat is a sandy brown color, with both reddish and darker markings.

EARS
The ears are large and low-set. They are able to detect the high-pitched calls of rodents, which cannot be heard by human ears, and the sound of feet scurrying across the desert sand.

PROFILE
This cat has a low-set body, with a broad head and a large nose.

MARKINGS
Stripes extend back from the eyes, and a dark area marks the back. The tail is ringed.

HOW BIG IS IT?

DANGEROUS LIVING
Many kinds of animals prey on sand cats, including birds of prey, wolves, and *venomous* (poisonous) snakes.

Silence and speed are vital to catching desert rodents.

Caracal (Persian Lynx)

SPECIES • *Caracal caracal*

These big cats get their name from the black tufts of hair on their ears. The name *caracal* comes from the Turkish word *karakulak,* meaning *black ears.*

VITAL STATISTICS

Weight	24–44 lb (11–20 kg); males are heavier
Length	32–55 in (80–140 cm); about 20 in (50 cm) tall
Sexual Maturity	About 21 months
Length of Pregnancy	63–75 days
Number of Offspring	Averages 2–3, but can be up to 6; weaning occurs at around 45 days
Diet	Hunts a range of small mammals, as well as birds and lizards
Lifespan	11–12 years in the wild; up to 17 in captivity

ANIMAL FACTS

Caracals *(KAR uh kals)* are remarkably agile, even for cats. They can jump vertically to catch small birds, but they are also strong enough to overpower antelope more than twice their size. If threatened, they can climb to safety. Until recently in India, people would release a caracal into a group of pigeons. Then they would bet on how many of the birds the caracal could knock down in a single leap.

The long, black tufts on the caracal's ears are also called tassels.

WHERE IN THE WORLD?

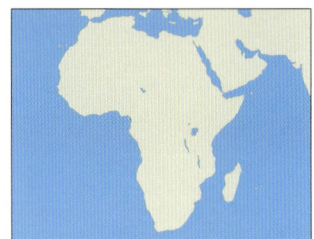

Ranges widely in Africa, outside the Sahara and central rain forest belt, and across the Arabian Peninsula into Turkey and east through Asia to India.

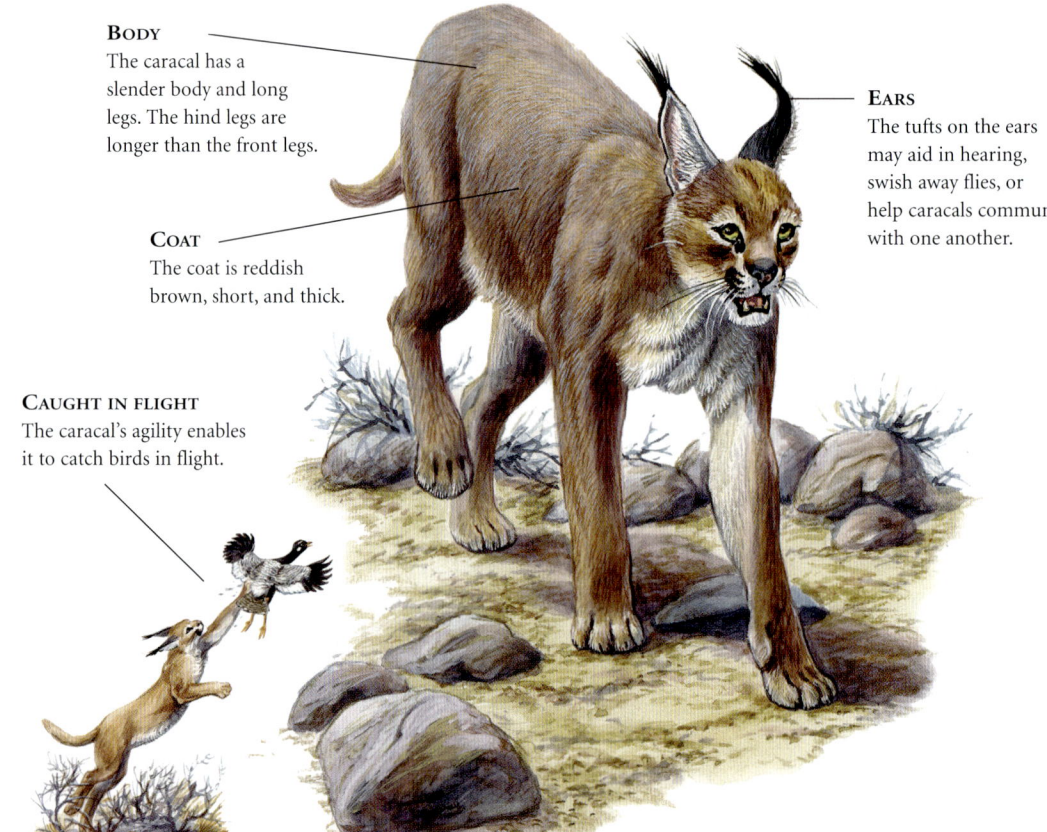

Body
The caracal has a slender body and long legs. The hind legs are longer than the front legs.

Coat
The coat is reddish brown, short, and thick.

Ears
The tufts on the ears may aid in hearing, swish away flies, or help caracals communicate with one another.

Caught in flight
The caracal's agility enables it to catch birds in flight.

HOW BIG IS IT?

SLEEPING ARRANGEMENTS

A caracal rests under a rock. These cats may be active during the day or night and are solitary by nature.

Aardwolf

SPECIES • *Proteles cristatus*

VITAL STATISTICS	
WEIGHT	20–31 lb (9–14 kg)
LENGTH	30–43 in (75–110 cm), including tail; up to 20 in (50 cm) tall
SEXUAL MATURITY	About 2 years
LENGTH OF PREGNANCY	90–110 days
NUMBER OF OFFSPRING	1–5, averaging 2–3; weaning occurs at 4 months
DIET	Feeds mainly on termites; occasionally eats small mammals and birds
LIFESPAN	10–12 years in the wild; up to 15 in captivity

The unusual name of the aardwolf comes from an Afrikaans word, which translates as *earth wolf*, referring to the way in which these animals *burrow* (dig). Aardwolves are the smallest type of hyena.

WHERE IN THE WORLD?

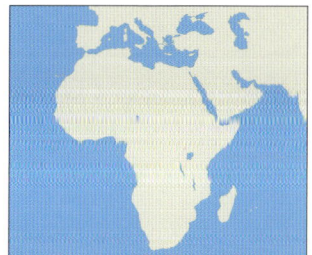

Lives in three widely spaced regions of Africa: in the east around the Horn of Africa; across southern parts; and in the central area.

ANIMAL FACTS

The feeding habits of the aardwolf are very specific. The animal lives only in grassland and savanna areas where harvester termites can be found. The aardwolf breaks open termite mounds using the sharp claws on its front feet. It then drags out the termites using its long, sticky tongue. An aardwolf can eat up to 200,000 insects at one time. But an aardwolf never destroys a *colony* (group). That allows the animal to return to feed there again. Aardwolves come out only at night and so are seldom seen.

APPEARANCE
Black vertical stripes run down the sides of the body.

EARS
The large ears help to detect prey.

MANE
The mane extends down the neck and back and can be raised to make the aardwolf look more fearsome.

LEGS
The body of this hyena slopes down to the hindquarters because the front legs are longer than the hind legs.

HOUSEKEEPING

Aardwolves establish certain areas in their *territories* (personal areas) for eliminating their waste. They dig a hole, then cover the hole after urinating or defecating in it (below left). They mark their territory by spreading musky material on grass stalks (below right).

Aardwolves display individual patterning.

HOW BIG IS IT?

28 MAMMALS

Greater Bilby

SPECIES • *Macrotis lagotis*

VITAL STATISTICS	
WEIGHT	2–5 lb (0.9–2.3 kg)
LENGTH	11–22 in (29–55 cm); tail is ¾ the body length
SEXUAL MATURITY	Females 6 months; males 8 months
LENGTH OF PREGNANCY	13–16 days
NUMBER OF OFFSPRING	1–2, occasionally 3; young spend 75 days in the pouch and are independent by 90 days
DIET	Eats insects, spiders, and worms; also bulbs and seeds
LIFESPAN	5–7 years

This *species* (kind) is the largest of the group of mammals called bandicoots. The greater bilby is also known as the pinkie because of the color of its nose.

WHERE IN THE WORLD?

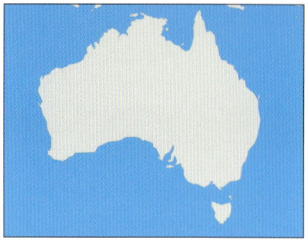

Now confined to Western Australia, Northern Territory, and southwestern Queensland.

ANIMAL FACTS

The range of these marsupials is directly affected by the soil because of the animal's need to tunnel. The species is often found in scrubland areas, where it can dig *burrows* (underground shelters) with relative ease. These retreats shield them from the hot sun and provide a refuge from *predators* (hunting animals). They are only temporary homes, however. Bilbys move on and dig a new home when food becomes scarce. They live singly or sometimes in pairs, shuffling along slowly when walking.

While the front toes (left) are about the same size, there is a much larger toe on each hind foot (right).

TUNNELING
A spiraling tunnel leads to a sleeping chamber around 5 feet (1.5 meters) below the surface.

NOSE
The nose is pink, with prominent whiskers.

TAIL
The banded tail is gray at the base, black in the middle, and white at the tip.

EARS
Long and pointed, the ears help the greater bilby to hear well. Hearing is an important sense for the animal, as its eyesight is poor.

GROOMING
The claws on the hind feet are used for grooming.

HOW BIG IS IT?

SLEEPING
This bandicoot puts its muzzle between its front paws, covers its eyes with its ears, and sleeps standing up.

Red Kangaroo

SPECIES • *Macropus rufus*

VITAL STATISTICS	
Weight	37–187 lb (82–412 kg); males are bigger
Length	4.3–9.5 ft (1.3–2.9 m) including tail.
Sexual Maturity	Females 14–20 months; males about 20 months
Length of Pregnancy	33–34 days
Number of Offspring	1; the joey spends around 235 days in the pouch
Diet	Grazes almost entirely on grass
Lifespan	Up to 15 years in the wild; 18 in captivity

ANIMAL FACTS

Kangaroos are well suited to living in a hot environment. They become active toward dusk when temperatures fall. Their fur is short, which helps them to stay cool. Kangaroos are *marsupials* (mammals that give birth to tiny young, which finish growing in the mother's pouch). After a *joey* (youngster) is born, the mother often mates again. However, the *embryo* (unborn young) formed from this mating does not develop into a joey until after the first joey finishes nursing.

Kangaroos usually have one offspring at a time.

The red kangaroo is the largest kangaroo, with males standing up to 6 feet (1.8 meters) tall. Red kangaroos can jump 30 feet (9.1 meters) in a single bound.

WHERE IN THE WORLD?

Ranges across most of the interior of Australia but is absent from coastal areas.

HINDQUARTERS
The muscular hindquarters allow large kangaroos to bound along at speeds of up to 30 miles (48 kilometers) per hour for short distances.

TAIL
The heavy tail of these kangaroos measures over 3 feet (1 meter) long in adults.

BOXING
Males may challenge each other in boxing contests, often jabbing with their front legs and lashing out with their hind legs.

EYES
Kangaroos can see in almost a full circle because of the position of their eyes. Their wide field of vision helps them spot potential dangers in open countryside.

RUNNING POSTURE
The kangaroo runs with its head low and forelegs bent backward.

HOW BIG IS IT?

IN THE POUCH
The young joey suckles on one of its mother's teats within the pouch.

Yellow-Footed Rock Wallaby

SPECIES • *Petrogale xanthopus*

This is one of the most brightly colored members of the kangaroo family. Its population is declining, and it is now among the rarest.

VITAL STATISTICS

Weight	6–20 lb (2.7–9 kg); males are bigger
Length	18–25 in (48–65 cm), including tail, which is almost as long as the body
Sexual Maturity	Females 18–24 months; males about 20 months
Length of Pregnancy	30–34 days
Number of Offspring	1; the joey spends around 250 days in the pouch
Diet	Eats grass and other plant matter, including bark
Lifespan	12–18 years

WHERE IN THE WORLD?

Lives in eastern Australia, from southwestern Queensland down through western New South Wales to South Australia.

ANIMAL FACTS

Rock wallabies live in *colonies* (groups) of up to 100 individuals in rocky environments. The wallaby's breeding cycle is strongly influenced by the availability of food. During periods of drought, they can delay the development of any *embryo* (unborn young) in the female's body. Only after conditions improve will the pregnancy proceed. These wallabies have become endangered, mostly because of competition with introduced goats and sheep.

Upperparts
These are gray, with a blackish band extending from the nose and encircling the eyes.

Hind feet
The soles of their hind feet have grooved skin, helping the animals grip rock surfaces. When hopping across rocks, rock wallabies carry their tail arched above the back.

Tail
The tail is long and does not taper significantly along its length. It is striped, with a dark tip.

A wallaby can leap across rocky surfaces with ease, holding its front legs at right angles to steady itself.

HOW BIG IS IT?

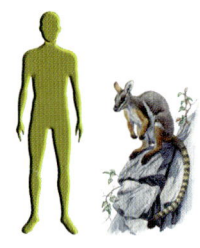

DANGER ABOVE
Although they can outrun would-be *predators* (hunting animals) on the ground, wallabies are at risk from birds of prey.

Honey Badger

SPECIES • *Mellivora capensis*

The honey badger has a misleading name. It is not a true badger, though it looks and behaves like one. Also called the *ratel*, honey badgers eat small animals, though honey is their preferred food.

VITAL STATISTICS

WEIGHT	12–31 lb (5.5–14 kg); males are heavier
LENGTH	About 30 in (76 cm); up to 12 in (30 cm) tall
SEXUAL MATURITY	2–3 years
LENGTH OF PREGNANCY	42–56 days; development may not start directly after fertilization in northern areas
NUMBER OF OFFSPRING	Average 2, ranges from 1–4; weaning occurs at around 1 year
DIET	Preys on insects, fish, reptiles, amphibians, and mammals up to the size of antelopes
LIFESPAN	3–11 years; up to 26 in captivity

ANIMAL FACTS

Honey badgers have a remarkable partnership with a type of bird called the honey guide. The call of a honey guide leads the honey badger to a beehive. The honey badger then breaks open the nest. After the honey badger has finished eating, the honey guide darts in to eat the beeswax and bee *larvae* (immature bees).

WHERE IN THE WORLD?

Found throughout Africa, apart from the Sahara. It ranges across the Arabian Peninsula, east through southern parts of Asia to Turkmenistan and India.

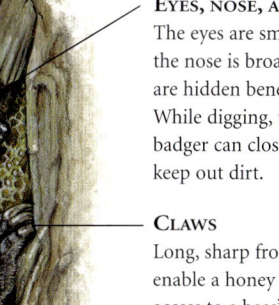

COAT AND TAIL
Thick and dense, the coat helps protect against the stings of angry bees. The tail is relatively short.

SMELL DEFENSE
Special glands give off a foul-smelling liquid that helps to discourage attackers.

EYES, NOSE, AND EARS
The eyes are small, and the nose is broad. The ears are hidden beneath the skin. While digging, the honey badger can close its ears to keep out dirt.

CLAWS
Long, sharp front claws enable a honey badger to gain access to a bees' nest easily.

DETERMINED NATURE
The honey badger has been called the most fearless animal in the world. It often intimidates creatures much larger than itself.

The claw can measure 1.6 inches (4 centimeters) long.

HOW BIG IS IT?

Cape Hyrax

SPECIES • *Procavia capensis*

Although it looks like a rodent, the Cape hyrax is actually more closely related to elephants. It descended from larger ancestors.

VITAL STATISTICS

WEIGHT	4–12 lb (1.8–5.4 kg)
LENGTH	17–21 in (44–54 cm)
SEXUAL MATURITY	After 16 months
LENGTH OF PREGNANCY	210–235 days
NUMBER OF OFFSPRING	1–4; births of the females in a group are synchronized, occurring within a period of 3 weeks; weaning occurs after 70 days
DIET	Grazes mainly on grass
LIFESPAN	Up to 12 years; females live longer than males

ANIMAL FACTS

Cape hyraxes, also called rock hyraxes, live in groups of up to seven related females. They often huddle together to keep warm because they are not able to regulate their body temperature as effectively as most mammals. Cape hyraxes also bask in the sun as a way of raising their body temperature. Males are territorial. A single male lives with a group of many females. Births are timed to occur during the rainy season, when food is most plentiful.

Cape hyraxes have a distinctive brown scent gland on their backs.

WHERE IN THE WORLD?

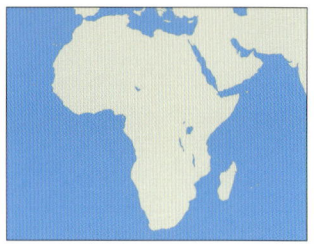

Lives in rocky areas across much of Africa, particularly in the mountainous parts of the Sahara and Namib deserts, extending eastward to the Arabian Peninsula.

FACIAL FEATURES
The rounded ears are set low. The nose is black, and the eyes are dark, surrounded by pale fur.

LONG HAIRS
Distributed randomly over the body, these long hairs resemble whiskers and have a similar sensory function.

SCENT GLAND
Cape hyraxes use the scent from the gland to communicate with one another and to mark their *territory* (personal area).

TEETH
The *incisors* (cutting teeth) are enlarged and resemble small tusks. They project over the lower lip.

HIND FEET
These are equipped with a sharp inner claw.

HOW BIG IS IT?

DANGER OVERHEAD

Living in rocky areas means that these mammals must climb well. They are vulnerable to birds of prey from overhead.

Black-Tailed Jack Rabbit

SPECIES • *Lepus californicus*

VITAL STATISTICS	
Weight	5–12 lb (2.2–5.5 kg); females are heavier
Length	18–30 in (46–76 cm)
Sexual Maturity	May be mature by 7 months, but do not breed until the following year
Length of Pregnancy	41–47 days
Number of Offspring	1–6, typically 3; weaning occurs by 28 days; females may have up to 6 litters per year
Diet	Eats grass, herbs, and twigs
Lifespan	Up to 5 years

This desert-dwelling *species* (kind) is a hare rather than a rabbit. It is able to twist and turn quickly, and it can even swim away from danger.

WHERE IN THE WORLD?

Ranges through the western and central United States, east to Texas and south into northern Mexico as well as Baja California. Introduced to Kentucky, New Jersey, and Nantucket Island.

ANIMAL FACTS

Life in relatively open country poses particular dangers to the black-tailed jack rabbit. The animal is an obvious target for a host of *predators* (hunting animals). As a result, these hares tend to rest during the day and become active toward dusk. Although they are solitary by nature, jack rabbits may feed in groups. They can run at speeds of up to 45 miles (72 kilometers) per hour. They are able to jump as far as 19 feet (6 meters) in a single bound.

The ears of the black-tailed jack rabbit reach 4.25 inches (11 centimeters) long.

Eyes
Keen eyesight helps these animals stay alert to potential danger.

Coloration
The animal has brownish-black upperparts and white underparts.

Ears
Sound travels over long distances in the desert, and the large ears help detect noises. They also help the hare to stay cool.

Recognition
The distinctive feature of this species is the black stripe extending down the tail.

Hind legs
These are strong and powerful, enabling the hare to run quickly.

HOW BIG IS IT?

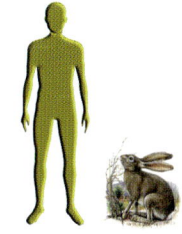

FORMS
These jack rabbits do not dig *burrows* (underground shelters) the way rabbits do. Instead, they rest in holes, known as *forms*, that they dig in the ground.

Hamadryas Baboon

SPECIES • *Papio hamadryas*

VITAL STATISTICS	
Weight	20–47 lb (9–21.5 kg); males are about twice as heavy as females
Length	39–54 in (99–137 cm) overall; tail can be as long as the body
Sexual Maturity	Females 4.3 years; males 4.8–7 years
Length of Pregnancy	172 days
Number of Offspring	1; weaning occurs at 6–15 months
Diet	Eats a variety of foods, including plant matter, fruit, and small animals
Lifespan	Up to 38 years

These adaptable monkeys live in harsh desert environments, favoring rocky areas where they can climb. They will not stray far from water.

WHERE IN THE WORLD?

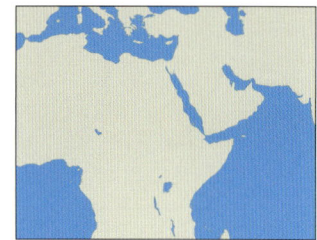

Lives in eastern Africa, in parts of Ethiopia, Somalia, and Eritrea, extending to the Middle East, in Saudi Arabia and Yemen.

FAMILY LIFE
Hamadryas baboons live in harems composed of one male and several females and their young. A large number of harems band together to form large groups. The males are fierce fighters and protect the group.

Males — Males are large, with a silvery mane on the head.

Females — Females are olive brown and lack any mane. Unlike other baboons, both male and female hamadryas baboons have a pink rump.

Tail — The tail is long and curved. Its length varies between individuals.

Young — These baboons have black fur at birth, which becomes olive brown beginning at about six months of age.

ANIMAL FACTS
Young baboons are totally dependent on their mothers, who carry them around. Males develop slowly, but are usually able to mate before their fur changes completely to its adult color. The baboons communicate using sounds as well as body language. Yawning, which exposes the *canine* (tearing) teeth, is considered a threatening gesture.

The hamadryas baboon is a *primate* (a group of mammals made up of human beings, apes, and monkeys).

HOW BIG IS IT?

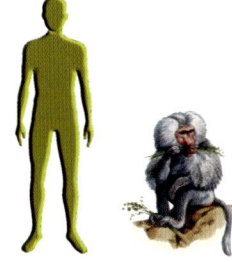

MATING
The *dominant* (ruling) male will chase, attack, and bite a female in the group who shows an interest in younger males.

Secretary-Bird

SPECIES • *Sagittarius serpentarius*

VITAL STATISTICS	
WEIGHT	7.3 lb (3.3 kg)
LENGTH	4.5 ft (140 cm); wingspan 4–5 ft (1.2–1.4 m); 4.1 ft (130 cm) tall
SEXUAL MATURITY	4 years
NUMBER OF EGGS	2, occasionally 3, pale green in color; male offspring may kill each other
INCUBATION PERIOD	About 45 days; flight occurs at 65–80 days
DIET	Eats snakes, lizards, rodents, eggs, and birds, as well as locusts and other animals without backbones
LIFESPAN	10–15 years; 20 in captivity

The name of this bird may come from the Arabic word *sekareteur*, meaning *hunter bird*. But the bird also has a crest of feathers that resemble the *quill* (feather) pens secretaries once carried behind their ears.

WHERE IN THE WORLD?

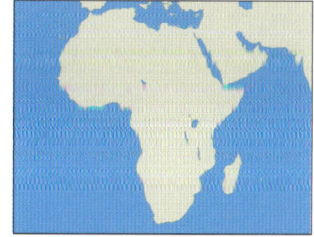

Restricted to Africa, south of the Sahara.

ANIMAL FACTS
Secretary-birds spend most of their time on the ground. Mates share a *territory* (personal area) but hunt independently and are usually seen apart. Snakes are a favorite prey. The bird grabs the snake by the neck and drops it from a height, to stun it. Then the bird jumps up and down on the snake's body while flapping its wings. This method of attack enables the birds to kill even *venomous* (poisonous) snakes with little risk of being bitten.

CREST FEATHERS
These are usually folded backward, extending over the nape of the neck.

TAIL
The tail has two long plumes.

LEGS
The legs are long, allowing the bird to take large strides as it walks. Its height also gives good visibility over a wide area.

TAKING TO THE AIR
The secretary-bird is also a good flier. It usually builds its nest at the top of a thorny acacia tree. The birds reuse their nests year after year.

THIGHS
Covered in black feathers, the long thighs enable the bird to sprint after prey. It may then attack with its feet and beak.

Both male and female secretary-birds spread their crest feathers during mating.

HOW BIG IS IT?

ON THE MOVE
Secretary-birds frequently walk more than 20 miles (32 kilometers) every day, looking for food. They also run fast.

Mediterranean Scorpion

SPECIES • *Buthus occitanus*

VITAL STATISTICS	
LENGTH	2.4–3.1 in (6–8 cm)
SEXUAL MATURITY	1–2 years
NUMBER OF EGGS	20–35
DEVELOPMENTAL PERIOD	Up to 8 months; young develop in the female's body
HABITAT	Dry rural areas, hiding under rocks; sometimes found in forests
DIET	Insects and other small animals
LIFESPAN	5–7 years

Although these scorpions are most common in warm areas, they are sometimes found at altitudes of more than 3,280 feet (1,000 meters).

WHERE IN THE WORLD?

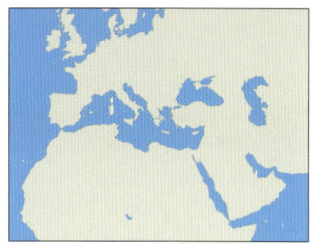

Lives throughout southwestern Europe, in France, Spain, and Portugal. Also lives across the Mediterranean, in North Africa.

ANIMAL FACTS

Scorpions have a flattened body, which enables them to squeeze into cracks and hide under desert rocks. The males of this *species* (kind) travel more widely than females, seeking mates. Newborn scorpions, called *scorplings,* are white at birth. They cling to their mother's body for several weeks until they grow a new outer skeleton and can live on their own. The strength of this scorpion's *venom* (poison) varies by where it lives. In Europe, the sting of this scorpion is unpleasant but usually not dangerous. However, the scorpions from North Africa have a much more powerful sting. The venom can sicken or in rare cases even kill a person.

STING
The scorpion's sting is located at the tip of the tail. It is brought forward over the head to subdue prey being held down by the claws.

ABDOMEN
Unlike insects, scorpions have just two body segments—the thorax, which includes the head, and the abdomen.

SCENTING SKILL
Scorpions have feathery sense organs called *pectines*. These structures, which trail on the ground, help the animal to sense vibrations and scents.

PEDIPALPS
These large pinchers are used to catch prey. They are covered with hair-like *setae*, which detect the movement of air made by moving prey.

HOW BIG IS IT?

WHAT DOSE?
Scorpions have a remarkable ability to match the amount of venom that they inject with the size of their prey.

Mexican Red-Kneed Tarantula

SPECIES • *Brachypelma smithi*

VITAL STATISTICS	
Weight	0.06–0.2 lb (27–90 g)
Length	5–5.5 in (12.7–14.0 cm)
Sexual Maturity	5–7 years
Hatching Period	2–8 weeks; young split up when they are 2–3 weeks old
Number of Eggs	Around 400, which are laid in an egg sac by the female
Diet	Hunts amphibians, rodents, reptiles, and small birds
Lifespan	Males live about 5 years, but females may have a lifespan of 25–50 years

Although many tarantulas live in rain forests, the Mexican red-kneed tarantula lives in desert areas of central America. It hides in a *burrow* (underground shelter) during the day and hunts small prey at night.

WHERE IN THE WORLD?

Restricted to the Pacific coastal area of Mexico.

ANIMAL FACTS

Territorial and solitary, these large spiders live in burrows. The relative humidity in burrows is much higher than that above ground, with dew forming each day at the burrow's entrance. This dew provides the tarantula with fluid to avoid fatal dehydration. At night, the tarantula emerges to hunt. The tarantula uses the tips of its legs to help it sense its surroundings in the dark. The number of these tarantulas has fallen, partly because many were taken as pets. Now, the pet trade uses tarantulas that were bred in captivity.

Urticating hairs
Tarantulas defend themselves using tiny, barbed hairs called *urticating hairs*. By rubbing their hind legs together, they can fling thousands of these hairs from their abdomen. The hairs can cause intense irritation, especially if they get into the eyes.

Markings
Exact patterning differs somewhat between individuals.

Eye cluster
These tarantulas have eight eyes, looking both forward and back, though their vision is not good.

Mouthparts
These tarantulas can inflict a painful bite to overcome prey rapidly. To people, the bite feels like a wasp sting.

Tarantulas will challenge and fight intruders.

HOW BIG IS IT?

OVERCOMING PREY
If a tarantula can sink its fangs into its victim, it will win the battle, even if the other animal is larger.

38 ARACHNIDS

Trap-Door Spider

FAMILY • Mygalomorphae

VITAL STATISTICS	
Length	0.63–0.90 in (1.6–2.3 cm); females larger
Sexual Maturity	Within a year
Hatching Period	Young hatch in mother's burrow and live there for some time
Number of Eggs	Likely to be 50–100
Habitat	Areas where burrows can be dug easily
Diet	Mainly insects
Lifespan	Probably 1–3 years

These spiders do not build large webs. Instead, they hide under trap doors in their *burrows* (underground shelters) and ambush passing prey, dragging them into their underground lairs.

WHERE IN THE WORLD?

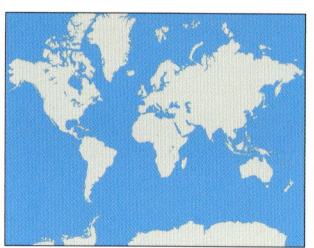

Can be found in much of South America; southern Africa and Madagascar; the Iberian Peninsula; Asia except the far north; and Australia and New Zealand.

ANIMAL FACTS

These spiders may build an internal door in their burrow to help protect against flooding during periods of heavy rainfall. The burrow itself slopes backward underground. In some cases, the entrance to the tunnel may look like a simple worm hole. A number of these spiders often live close to one another. They can inhabit forested areas, but they also hunt in home gardens in some areas.

TRAP DOOR
The trap door that covers the entrance to the burrow is made of silk and mud. It is attached to the lining of the burrow by silk hinges.

COLORATION
These spiders are mainly brown, with a long body.

BITE
Trap-door spiders can inflict a painful bite, but it usually does no lasting harm to people. Males, which spend more time out of their burrows than females, can be aggressive.

LEGS
The limbs are strong, helping the spider to move at great speed. They also help the spider to overpower its prey.

When the spider bites an insect, poison squirts through the fangs into the wound to paralyze or kill the victim.

HOW BIG IS IT?

HUNTING STRATEGIES

The spider waits under its door until prey walks by. Then it quickly opens the door, seizes and poisons its victim, and drags it into the burrow.

ARACHNIDS 39

Crab Spider

FAMILY • Thomisidae

The pretty colors of the crab spider serve a deadly purpose. They enable these spiders to ambush and catch their prey by hiding in flowers.

VITAL STATISTICS

LENGTH	Males 0.11–0.16 in (0.3–0.4 cm); females 0.35–0.39 in (0.9–1 cm)
SEXUAL MATURITY	6 months
HATCHING PERIOD	2 weeks for the eggs to hatch in their egg sac
NUMBER OF EGGS	Typically 45–500, depending on the species; sometimes guarded by the female
HABITAT	Varies, from desert to grassland
DIET	Such insects as bees, butterflies, and hoverflies, which are attracted to flowers
LIFESPAN	1 year or less

WHERE IN THE WORLD?

Crab spiders live on every continent except Antarctica.

ANIMAL FACTS

Crab spiders do not spin webs to catch their prey. Instead, they hunt by waiting on flowers to ambush unsuspecting insects. Their eyes serve as motion sensors, alerting them to the presence of prey. Crab spiders can overcome creatures larger than themselves, thanks to their potent *venom* (poison). Unlike some other spiders, these spiders do not store their prey once they have made a kill. Instead, they feed immediately.

Even stinging insects cannot escape the crab spider.

COLORATION
Crab spiders may spend several days slowly changing their color to match the the flower they are hiding on.

BODY SHAPE
The short, wide body is similar to that of a crab.

EYES
The small eyes detect motion and are critical in helping these spiders to locate prey.

LEGS
The first two pairs of legs are the longest. The spiders keep these legs apart to catch prey. Crab spiders can walk backward, forward, or sideways.

HOW BIG IS IT?

DIFFERENT STRATEGIES

A crab spider can lower itself into the pitcher of an insect-eating plant to seize an insect that has fallen inside.

Southern Black Widow

SPECIES • *Latrodectus mactans*

Black widows got their name because people saw the female spiders killing males after mating. However, such killings occur in only a few *species* (kinds) of black widows.

VITAL STATISTICS

LENGTH	0.3–0.4 in (0.8–1.0 cm); males are about half the size of females
SEXUAL MATURITY	About 3 months
HATCHING PERIOD	Young hatch in the egg case after 3 weeks, emerging 2–4 weeks later
NUMBER OF EGGS	100–300 per batch; females lay several in succession
HABITAT	May venture into homes
DIET	Feeds mainly on insects and spiders
LIFESPAN	Males 1–2 months; females up to 3 years

ANIMAL FACTS

The black widow can be found in grasslands and forests, but it also lives in urban areas, where it often seeks shelter in buildings. It tends to live on its own. Male black widows are less dangerous than females and are several times smaller. The male approaches a female cautiously when seeking to mate, tapping out a special code on the female spider's silk web so he is not seen as prey. After hatching, fewer than 1 in 10 spiderlings survives. The rest are eaten by their siblings.

The shape of the spider's leg

WHERE IN THE WORLD?

Lives chiefly in the southeastern United States, though they can be found in almost every part of the United States.

LEGS
The tips of the legs are coated with a nonstick substance to prevent the spider from getting caught in its own web.

APPEARANCE
A female black widow is easily identified by her shiny black body and pattern of red markings. Males are more brightly colored.

PAINFUL BITE
The bite of a southern black widow is rarely fatal, though the spider's *venom* (poison) can cause illness and severe pain. Most bites occur when the animal becomes frightened.

EGG SAC
White to tan in color, the egg sac has a paper-like texture and protects the eggs inside it.

HOW BIG IS IT?

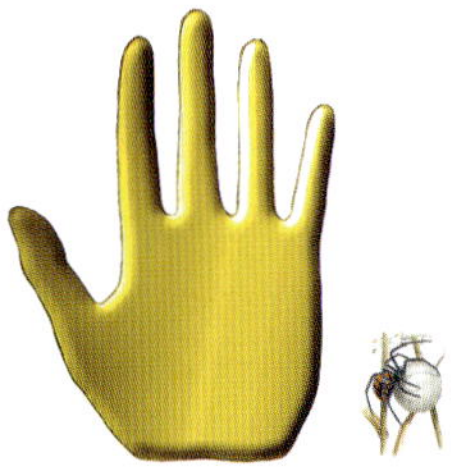

FEARSOME KILLER CLOSE-UP
The spider injects its venom with its sharp, hard, hollow fangs. An opening at the tip of the fang connects to the poison *glands* (organs).

Dung Beetle

GENUS • *Scarabaeus*

VITAL STATISTICS	
Length	0.12–2 in (0.3–5 cm), depending on species
Sexual Maturity	After it becomes a pupa
Number of Eggs	Up to 3 per day
Development Period	Life cycle takes 5–16 weeks
Habitat	Open countryside, especially where there are herds of plant-eating mammals
Diet	Feeds on dung, even extracting water from it
Lifespan	Adults live 2–6 months

Dung beetles are important recyclers. They play a vital role in breaking down animal *dung* (solid waste) and returning its *nutrients* (nourishing substances) to the soil.

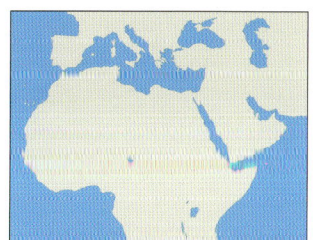

WHERE IN THE WORLD?

Lives on all continents except Antarctica.

ANIMAL FACTS

There are thousands of *species* (kinds) of dung beetle spread all around the world. A strong sense of smell enables dung beetles to home in on their target. Some species hitch a ride on other animals, dropping off at the appropriate time to obtain a meal. Some dung beetles live in and on dung piles. Others live in tunnels they have dug into the dung. Still others, called rollers, carve out a portion of dung and shape it into a ball called a brood ball. A roller moves the brood ball by standing on its front legs and pushing the ball with its hind legs. It buries the brood ball to eat later or to use as a place to lay eggs.

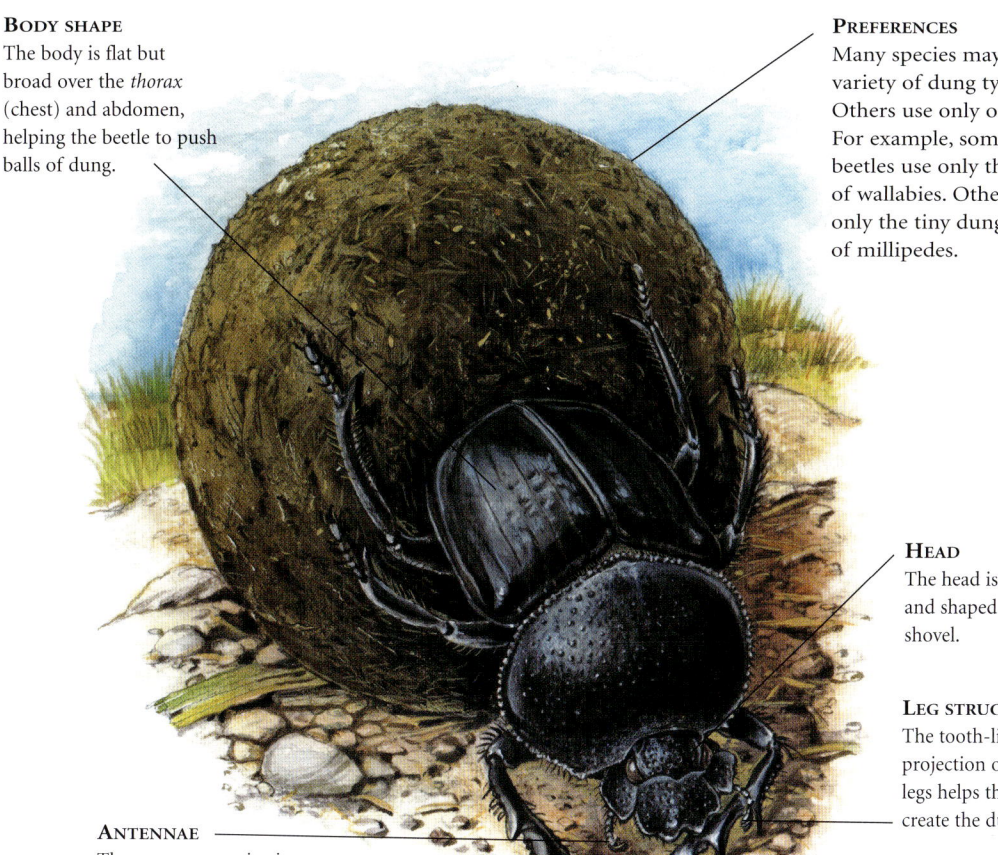

Body shape
The body is flat but broad over the *thorax* (chest) and abdomen, helping the beetle to push balls of dung.

Preferences
Many species may use a variety of dung types. Others use only one type. For example, some dung beetles use only the dung of wallabies. Others use only the tiny dung pellets of millipedes.

Head
The head is flat and shaped like a shovel.

Leg structure
The tooth-like projection on the front legs helps the beetle create the dung ball.

Antennae
These sensory projections are small in dung beetles, ending in tufts.

HOW BIG IS IT?

BREEDING BEHAVIOR
A male and female will set off together with a ball of dung. After mating, the female lays her eggs in the brood ball.

Thorny Devil

SPECIES • *Moloch horridus*

VITAL STATISTICS	
Weight	12 oz (33–57 g); males are smaller
Length	3–4 in (8–10 cm)
Sexual Maturity	From about 3 years, before they have finished growing
Number of Eggs	3–10 per clutch; young eat their eggshells
Incubation Period	Typically 13–18 weeks, depending on temperature
Diet	Feed almost entirely on ants—up to 1,000 in a single meal
Lifespan	20 years

ANIMAL FACTS
The thorny devil can change color rapidly to match the soil it is walking on. Grooves on the animal's body and legs channel dew or any other water that lands on the animal to its mouth. Like other lizards, horny devils are cold-blooded—that is, the temperature of their body matches their surroundings. During the cold desert night, the lizards dig a hole and cover themselves with dirt to stay warm. After sunrise, thorny devils often bask on roads to warm up quickly. Unfortunately, this makes them vulnerable to being run over by vehicles.

These lizards are well protected against *predators* (hunting animals) by the variety of sharp projections covering their bodies. They look fearsome, but in fact they are not aggressive.

WHERE IN THE WORLD?

Lives throughout much of Australia.

Horns
Present above each eye, the horns may be a storage area for fat.

Spiked hump
This swollen area at the back of the head is a defensive weapon. When threatened, the lizards put their head between their front legs. The hump becomes a false head that draws attention away from the real head.

Unaffected by the sting
These lizards feed almost entirely on ants. They may ambush the insects outside the nest. The lizards seem to be immune to ant *venom* (poison).

Legs
Protected by sharp spines, the legs are also equipped with sharp claws.

Appearance
The body is covered in a random array of spikes, offering protection and camouflage.

HOW BIG IS IT?

DEFENSIVE POSTURE
The thorny devil uses the hump on its head to protect itself from dingoes and other potential predators.

Gila Monster

SPECIES • *Heloderma suspectum*

VITAL STATISTICS	
WEIGHT	2.9–5 lb (1.3–2.3 kg); the heaviest are found in the U.S.
LENGTH	12–24 in (30–60 cm); males are much larger
SEXUAL MATURITY	3–5 years, depending on growth rate
NUMBER OF EGGS	2–12, average 5
INCUBATION PERIOD	Around 9 months
DIET	Mainly the eggs of birds and reptiles; will also eat small mammals
LIFESPAN	20 years; up to 30 in captivity

The Gila *(hee-la)* monster is one of the few *venomous* (poisonous) lizards in the world. Gila monster bites are painful, but the venom is not fatal to adults.

WHERE IN THE WORLD?

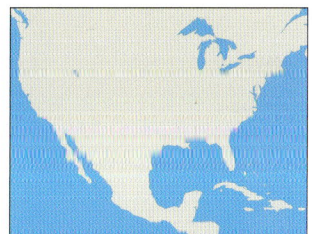

Found chiefly in the Sonoran Desert of the southwestern United States and northern Mexico.

ANIMAL FACTS

The Gila monster uses its powerful venom mainly to defend itself against *predators* (hunting animals). Like many reptiles, Gila monsters can eat large meals, up to about one-third of their body weight. This *adaptation* (characteristic) helps them to survive in areas where food is hard to find. Gila monsters move slowly but can travel long distances. They spend most of their time underground and *hibernate* (enter a sleep-like state) during the winter. They can climb well if they need to.

TAIL
This is used to store fat, allowing the lizard to go for months without eating.

FRONT FEET
These are strong and tipped with powerful claws to help the lizard dig.

A DEADLY BITE
The venom is released along grooves in the teeth of the lower jaw. When the lizard bites a victim, these grooves carry venom into the wound.

SCALES
These resemble beads of different colors, including black, pink, orange, and yellow.

ON THE SCENT
Gila monsters have a sharp sense of smell that helps them to find hidden prey.

HOW BIG IS IT?

Shingle-Backed Lizard

SPECIES • *Tiliqua rugosa*

VITAL STATISTICS	
Weight	1.8 lb (0.8 kg)
Length	12–18 in (30–45 cm)
Sexual Maturity	3 years
Incubation Period	About 5 months
Number of Offspring	1–2, occasionally 3, measuring about 6 in (15 cm) at birth
Diet	Eat flowers, fruits, and vegetation; also animal remains
Lifespan	20–30 years

These skinks get their name from their unusual appearance. The large pine-cone-shaped scales on the upper surface of their body are arranged like overlapping shingles on a roof.

WHERE IN THE WORLD?

Lives only in Australia, mainly in southern and western parts of the continent.

ANIMAL FACTS

Shingle-backed lizards are skinks—small, smooth-scaled lizards with short, weak legs or no legs at all. After a cold night in the desert, these lizards often bask on highways in the morning to raise their body temperature. They do not run from danger but instead curve their body into the shape of a C and hiss, exposing their blue tongue. Pairs tend to stay together. A male relies on his sense of smell to detect when the female is ready to mate. Eggs develop inside the female's body. They hatch and the young are born live.

SCALES
These are large and stick out from the body, explaining why this species is also called the pinecone skink.

HEAD
Triangular in shape, the head resembles a rock, apart from the black eyes.

TONGUE
Shingle-backed lizards expose their bright blue tongue when they are threatened.

TAIL
The tail is shaped like the head, which can confuse would-be *predators* (hunting animals).

A FREE MEAL
By scavenging animals killed on highways, the slow-moving lizards risk becoming victims themselves.

HOW BIG IS IT?

Although they live in a dry environment, shingle-backed lizards can swim well, using their legs to paddle along.

Western Diamondback Rattlesnake

SPECIES • *Crotalus atrox*

Rattlesnakes often make a rattling sound as a warning before they strike. These snakes remain numerous, despite the slaughter by hunters of thousands of the snakes in "rattlesnake roundups."

VITAL STATISTICS

WEIGHT	Average 15 lb (6.8 kg), but can be up to 23 lb (10.4 kg); males larger
LENGTH	Average 4 ft (1.2 m), but has reached 7 ft (2.13 m)
SEXUAL MATURITY	2–3 years
INCUBATION PERIOD	6–7 months
NUMBER OF OFFSPRING	About 12; they disperse shortly after birth, already venomous
DIET	Feeds mainly on rodents and rabbits; also some birds and lizards
LIFESPAN	Up to 22 years

ANIMAL FACTS

This *venomous* (poisonous) snake is one of the boldest and most aggressive of all rattlesnakes. The snakes hunt at night during the summer and *hibernate* (enter a sleep-like state) through winter, though they sometimes emerge on warmer winter days. The snakes retreat into caves or share the *burrows* (underground shelters) of other creatures at this time of year. These rattlesnakes sometimes survive for up to two years without eating if necessary, thanks to their stores of body fat.

The modified scales in the tail, called *beads*, vibrate against each other to create the rattle.

WHERE IN THE WORLD?

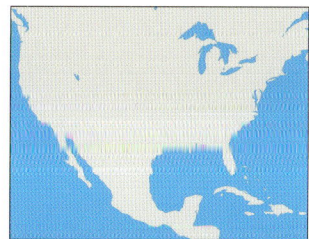

Extends from California across the United States to Arkansas, south into much of northern Mexico.

EYE STRIPE
This extends diagonally across the cheeks from below each eye.

BE ALARMED!
A rattlesnake may rest curled up in the open. If disturbed, it adopts a more menacing posture, with its head raised to strike.

BITES
Although the bite of a western diamondback is painful and may cause serious damage, it is rarely fatal to human adults.

MARKINGS
The diamond pattern on their back explains their name.

RATTLE
The rattle is formed by horny pieces loosely joined together at the tip of the tail. The rattle gets larger as the snake ages.

SCALES
The scales are highly visible, despite their underlying coloration.

HOW BIG IS IT?

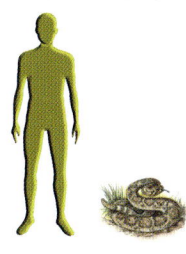

MATING
Mating occurs in spring. Males sometimes fight to win the right to mate with females.

Glossary

adaptation a characteristic of a living thing that makes it better able to survive and reproduce in its environment

adaptable behaving with flexibility and in a variety of ways

arachnid a member of a class of small, insect-like animals that have four pairs of legs but no wings or *antennae* (feelers). Their bodies are divided into two main parts, the abdomen and the cephalothorax, which consists of the head and the thorax joined together.

bird the only living animal with feathers

burrow underground shelter

canids members of the dog family

canine a long, pointed tooth near the front of the mouth used for tearing

cloven hoof a hoof divided into an even number of toes, usually two

colony a group of animals or plants of the same kind, living or growing together

desert a barren region of Earth's surface that receives little rainfall

domesticate to change an animal or plant from a wild to a tame state suitable for agriculture

dominant to be the highest rank member of a group

dung solid waste from the intestines of animals

ecosystem a group of animal and plant populations living together in the same environment and its *abiotic* (nonliving or physical) environment, including climate, soil, water, air, nutrients, and energy

embryo unborn young

extinction occurs when every member of a species of a living thing has died

forage search for

habitat the kind of place in which an animal lives

hibernation an inactive, sleep-like state that some animals enter during the winter

incisor a tooth having a sharp edge for cutting

insect a small, six-legged animal that as an adult has a body divided into three main parts—head, thorax, and abdomen—and a tough shell-like outer covering. Most insects also have wings and a pair of *antennae* (feelers).

joey a young kangaroo

lichen any of a group of living things that consist of a fungus and a simple organism growing together in a single unit

marsupial a mammal whose young are born in an extremely immature state. The newborn undergoes most of its development attached to one of its mother's nipples and is nourished by her milk. Marsupial females usually have a *marsupium* (pouch) to protect the babies.

mammal an animal that feeds its young on the mother's milk

nocturnal active at night

pack a number of animals of the same kind hunting or living together

pedipalp one of a pair of short, leg-like appendages near the mouth and fangs of spiders, used as aids in feeding and during breeding

predator an animal that preys upon other animals

primate a group of mammals made up of human beings, apes, and monkeys

reptile an animal that has dry, scaly skin and breathes with lungs

rodent a type of mammal with front teeth especially suited to gnawing hard objects

scavenge to feed on decaying matter

scrubland land overgrown with low, stunted trees or shrubs

species a group of animals or plants that have certain permanent characteristics in common and are able to interbreed

territory an area within definite boundaries, such as a nesting ground, in which an animal lives and from which it keeps out others of its kind

thorax also called the chest, the part of the body between the base of the neck and the abdomen

tubers underground stems

venom a poisonous substance produced by many kinds of animals to injure, kill, or digest prey

wean to accustom a young animal to food other than its mother's milk

Resources

Books

Desert Food Chains by Bobbie Kalman and Kelley MacAulay (Crabtree Publishing, 2005)
This book explains the food chains that provide energy to different desert animals.

The Sahara Desert: The Biggest Desert by Aileen Weintraub (PowerKids Press, 2001)
Explore the landforms and environment of the world's largest desert.

A Walk in the Desert by Rebecca L. Johnson and Phyllis V. Saroff (Carolrhoda Books, 2001)
Learn about the ways in which animals, plants, climate, and soil interact to create a desert habitat.

Websites

About Desert Animals: The Living Desert
http://www.livingdesert.org/desert_animals.html
Go in-depth with desert animals and plants at this website from the Living Desert Zoo and Botanical Gardens in Palm Desert, California.

The Animal Spot: Desert Animals
http://www.desertanimals.net/index.html
Learn how many different types of animals have adapted to live in one of the world's harshest environments.

National Geographic: Deserts
http://environment.nationalgeographic.com/environment/habitats/desert-profile/
Photo galleries and articles reveal the beauties and the dangers of deserts at this website from the National Geographic Society.

What's It Like Where You Live? Desert
http://www.mbgnet.net/sets/desert/index.htm
Follow Emily and Roderick through the different types of deserts around the world.

Acknowledgments

Cover photograph: Nature Picture Library (Rolf Nussbaumer)

Illustrations: © Art-Tech

Photographs:

Abdul Rahman Al-Sikhan: 8

Dreamstime: 11 (S. Dunn), 12 (S. Ekernas), 16 (U. Ravbar), 31 (C. Chesser), 32 (S. Noakes), 35 (J. G. Swanepoel), 42 (J. Schulz)

FLPA: 9 (Ron Austing), 13 (C. & T. Stuart), 27 (G. Lacz), 28 (E. Woods), 36 (B. Borrell Casals), 38 (M. Imamori), 39 (M. Moffett)

Fotolia: 30 (Iofoto), 45 (R. Dodson)

Getty Images: 7 (E. R. Degginger)

Photos.com: 10, 14, 17, 18, 19, 20, 21, 24, 26, 29, 33, 34, 41, 43

Photoshot: 37 (NHPA)

Public Domain: 6

Fisher Queen: 25

Trisha M. Shears: 44

Stock.Xchng: 23 (H. Berkovich)

Thinkstock: 40

Webshots: 15 (T. Kogler), 22 (S. Tautkus)

Index

A
aardwolf, 27
adaptation, 4
African hunting dog, 24
African wild ass, 18
Arabian camel. *See* dromedary camel
Arabian oryx, 12
argali, 13
ass, African wild, 18

B
baboon, hamadryas, 34
Bactrian camel, 16
badger, honey, 31
bandicoot, 28
Barbary sheep, 11
beetle, dung, 41
bighorn sheep, 14
bilby, greater, 28
black-backed jackal, 21
black-tailed jack rabbit, 33
black widow, southern, 40
brood balls, 41
burrows, 4

C
camel: Bactrian, 16; dromedary or Arabian, 17
cape hyrax, 32
caracal, 26
cat, sand, 25
cloning, 15
coyote, 19
crab spider, 39

D
deserts, 4–5
diamondback rattlesnake, western, 45
dingo, 20
dog, African hunting, 24
donkey, 18; Poitou, 18
dorcas gazelle, 10
dromedary camel, 17
dung beetle, 41

E
Egyptian jerboa, lesser, 7

F
fennec fox, 4, 23
fox, fennec, 4, 23

G
gazelle, dorcas, 10
Gila monster, 5, 43
golden jackal, 22
greater bilby, 28
gundi, 6

H
hamadryas baboon, 34
hare, 33
honey badger, 31
honey guide, 31
hunting dog, African, 24
hyena, 27
hyrax, cape, 32

J
jackal: black-backed, 21; golden, 22
jack rabbit, black-tailed, 33
jerboa, lesser Egyptian, 7
jird, Libyan, 8

K
kangaroo, 30; red, 29

L
lesser Egyptian jerboa, 7
Libyan jird, 8
lizard, 5; shingle-backed, 44. *See also* Gila monster; thorny devil
lynx, Persian, 26

M
marsupials, 29
Mediterranean scorpion, 36
Mexican red-kneed tarantula, 37
mole rat, naked, 4, 9
monkey, 34
mouflon, 15
mountain sheep, 13

N
naked mole-rat, 4, 9

O
oryx, Arabian, 12

P
Persian lynx, 26
pinkie. *See* greater bilby
Poitou donkey, 18

R
rabbit, 5; black-tailed jack, 33
rat, naked mole-. *See* naked mole-rat
ratel. *See* honey badger
rattlesnake, western diamondback, 45
red kangaroo, 29
red-kneed tarantula, Mexican, 37
rock hyrax. *See* cape hyrax
rock wallaby, yellow-footed, 30

S
Sahara, 4
sand cat, 25
scorpion, Mediterranean, 36
scrublands, 5
secretary-bird, 35
sheep: agali or mountain, 13; Barbary, 11; bighorn, 14; mouflon, 15
shingle-backed lizard, 44
snake, 5; western diamondback rattle-, 45
southern black widow, 40
spider: crab, 39; southern black widow, 40; trap-door, 38. *See also* Mexican red-kneed tarantula

T
tarantula, Mexican red-kneed, 37
termite, 27
thorny devil, 42
trap-door spider, 38

V
venom, 5

W
wallaby, yellow-footed rock, 30
western diamondback rattlesnake, 45
wild ass, African, 18

Y
yellow-footed rock wallaby, 30